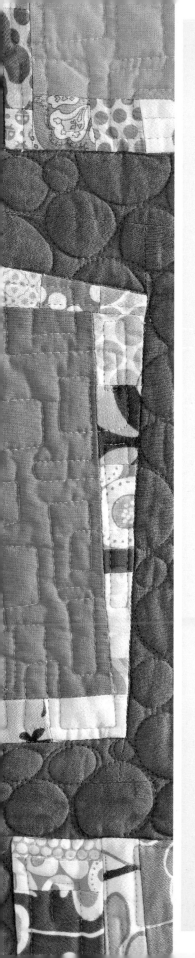

quilting modern

techniques and projects
for improvisational quilts

JACQUIE GERING

KATIE PEDERSEN

INTERWEAVE.
interweave.com

editor **Elaine Lipson**

technical editor **Rebecca Kemp Brent**

art director **Liz Quan**

designer **Julia Boyles**

illustrator **Missy Shepler**

photographer **Joe Hancock**

photo stylist **Julie Maldonado**

production designer **Katherine Jackson**

Interweave Press LLC
201 East Fourth Street
Loveland, CO 80537
interweave.com

Printed in China by C&C Offset

Library of Congress
Cataloging-in-Publication Data

Gering, Jacquie.

Quilting modern : techniques and
projects for improvisational quilts /
Jacquie Gering, Katie Pedersen.

    p. cm.

Includes bibliographical references and
index.

ISBN 978-1-59668-387-7 (pbk.)

1. Patchwork--Patterns. 2. Machine
quilting--Patterns. 3. Quilting I.
Pedersen, Katie. II. Title.

TT835.G33215 2012

746.46--dc23

2011039245

10 9 8 7 6 5 4 3 2 1

acknowledgments

Writing *Quilting Modern* has been a collaborative adventure and the best and longest blind date two people have ever had. Long days, intense conversations, and nose-to-the-grindstone work have resulted in a book we're proud to share and a friendship we cherish. The book is a product of our minds and hands and of each of you, our friends and family. You shared words of advice, put us in our place, propped us up, and sent us off to work with a smile and a cup of coffee. You know who you are, and we thank you.

from jacquie

People ask me if I come from an artistic family. I do. My sons, Ben and Jon, are musicians, but they didn't get their creative prowess from me, I got mine from them. Their out-of-the-box thinking, self-assurance, and willingness to dive into the creative process inspired me to become an artist. I can count on them for candid feedback, constant reminders to keep it modern, and not-so-gentle pushes out of my comfort zone. Standing right behind me cheering me on is my husband, Steve. I appreciate his strength, stability, calming influence, and listening ear. He would say he didn't get the creative gene, but he did. My mom and dad sent a few good genes my way along with some life lessons that have served me well. They taught me I could do whatever I set my mind to. Turns out, they were right. This book is for them.

from katie

Endless heartfelt thanks to my family. Roan, had it not been for you, I never would have discovered my love of quilting. Prefacing your questions with "Mama, when you finish that..." is hopefully at an end. Jeffrey, thanks for encouraging me to undertake this project, supporting me in every aspect of its completion, picking up where I had to leave off, and just plain loving me. You both are a daily dose of inspiration, and I promise someday to make the "livudio" more living room, less studio. Loving thanks to my parents for giving me my first sewing machine and for passing on your fondness for art and craft, including quilting. That love runs through my blood.

from jacquie and katie

So many of you have supported our journey as authors and encouraged us to persevere and write this book. Alissa, Noelle, and Cheryl, thank you for keeping secrets and sharing your experience and expertise. Kathy Mack, what would we have done without you? Your support, encouragement, and fabric supply made our lives easier. Thanks to the Warm Company, all of our quilts have batting. We love Warm and Natural. Robert Kaufman provided us with both prints and solids for the quilts. We're Kona solids fans forever! Aneela Hoey, Jan DiCintio, and Kerri Horsley provided fabrics for experimentation and to use in projects in the book. You're the best! Angela Walters, our longarm quilter, helped us bring our quilts to life. She is more than our quilter; she is an artist and our friend. When we asked, the quilting community responded. It's great when your friends have your back. Speaking of friends, thanks to our new Interweave friends for helping us realize our vision for *Quilting Modern*. We are grateful for your guidance and expertise along with some hand-holding and tough love. It's a beautiful book as you assured us it would be. Now, let's make some quilts!

contents

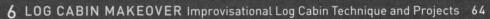

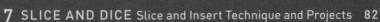
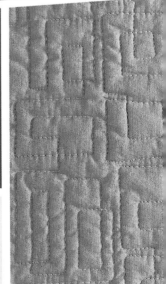

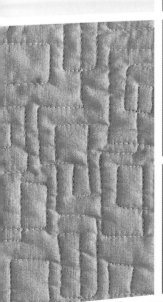

THE
improvisational
PATH

We wrote this book to share our designs for quilts with a modern aesthetic and our enthusiasm for improvisational quilting techniques. Improvisation has various interpretations, but for us it means creating in the moment and reacting to ideas and our environment to make something new. Improvisation energizes our creativity and fosters an inventive spirit.

In practice, improvising can be as simple as putting together a unique set of fabrics for your favorite quilt pattern, changing a traditional block, or putting a unique twist on a design; it can be as complex as setting out on your own with fabric and quilting tools.

A repertoire of techniques encourages and supports improvisation. The improvisational techniques are the heart of this book. We provide detailed instructions for each technique, followed by quilts or quilted projects that use that technique in different ways.

In the spirit of improvisation, here are a few principles that we try to live by.

honor the past. Take time to learn the rules of traditional quilting. The more you understand traditional methods, the easier it is to manipulate the rules to your benefit.

release your inner artist. Even if you've been told, or told yourself, that you are not an artist, there is an artist in you that you can cultivate and feed so that it blossoms. Surround yourself with art. Become an observer. View the world through an artistic eye.

embrace serendipity. Accidents happen all the time in the studio and are opportunities to see things in a different way. Recognize those happy accidents and capitalize on them.

fail. Improvisation is about trial and error. Cherish every mistake or misstep as a learning opportunity. Many of us don't start out of fear that we won't succeed. We recommend failing right from the start. Get it out of the way and move forward.

savor the moment. There are faster ways to make quilts than the methods in this book. Improvisation is about savoring every stitch, enjoying every moment, and making your own decisions. It's easier to let others do it for you, but the satisfaction from doing it yourself and making it your own is unparalleled.

make a friend. Through the process of writing this book, we've learned that neither of us is as good without the other as we are together. Open your process to the eyes of a friend. Enjoy the praise, but listen to the critique.

free yourself. We ask ourselves on a daily basis, what might happen if? Ideas are free for the taking. Grab one and take it where you want to go.

We will be flattered if you make the quilts in the book. We will be proud if you make them your own. Enjoy the journey.

Jacquie and Katie

tools and materials

FOR THE MODERN QUILTER

The right tools and materials make quilting easier and more fun. This book assumes that you have some basic knowledge of the standard tools and supplies of quiltmaking and sewing. Along with those, we recommend a few specific tools that we've found to support our improvisational piecing, sewing, and quilting methods and projects.

the modern quilter's toolbox

You'll need the following tools for every project in this book. Any additional tools that you'll need for specific projects, such as a zipper foot, are listed in the project instructions.

- Fabric scissors
- Thread clippers or small scissors
- Rotary cutters
- Dressmaker's shears
- Self-healing cutting mat
- Gridded acrylic quilter's rulers
- Straight pins
- Measuring tape
- Sewing machine with free-motion capability and walking foot attachment
- Seam ripper
- Design wall
- Blue painter's tape
- Quilter's safety pins

cutting

The success of your quilts depends, in part, on accurate cutting. It's important to have scissors with sharp blades that are designed for cutting fabric and that you reserve for that purpose. Sometimes using a rotary cutter instead of scissors is the most efficient strategy, so it's best to have both.

basic cutting tools

Our standard cutting tools include

- 24" × 36" (61 × 91.5 cm) self-healing cutting mat
- 45 mm rotary cutter
- 6" × 24" (15 × 61 cm) gridded acrylic quilter's ruler
- 8" (20.5 cm) dressmaker's shears for cutting fabric
- Small scissors or thread clippers for trimming threads
- Extra rotary cutter designated for cutting paper.

additional cutting tools

As you expand your supply kit, and as your budget allows, we recommend stocking up on extra cutting mats and other sizes of rulers. Extra cutting mats make improvisation easier. When working with panels or oversized blocks, they offer additional surface for squaring and cutting. Align several mats and tape them together on the underside to act as one large mat, or store an extra mat or two and take them out when needed.

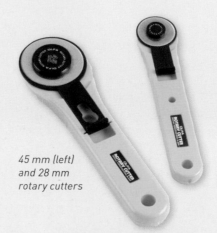

45 mm (left) and 28 mm rotary cutters

Longer rulers are helpful, too. Our ruler collection includes 36" (91.5 cm) and 48" (122 cm) rulers. You can often find inexpensive rulers at hardware stores, but remember that rulers made of wood or soft plastic can be damaged by a rotary cutter. Use only rigid acrylic or metal rulers when cutting with a rotary blade.

We also have a large collection of acrylic squaring rulers, from 2½" (6.5 cm) square to 15½" (39.5 cm) square, for fussy cutting (isolating a specific part of a print for cutting) and for measuring and trimming blocks. If you don't have the specific squaring ruler listed for a project, use a larger ruler and cut one or two sides of the block at a time, using the ruler gridlines to keep the corners square.

Finally, we keep a carpenter's square in our ruler box for squaring quilts.

sewing tools

The workhorses in our studio are our sewing machines, threads, and needles. Quality thread and needles make a difference in the quality of our work.

sewing machine

You'll need a basic sewing machine with straight-stitch capability to piece the quilts in the book. Zigzag and other decorative stitches are a bonus. To quilt your own quilts you need a walking foot attachment for straight-line quilting and a darning foot and the ability to drop the feed dog on your machine for free-motion quilting. Most machines come with a zipper foot, which you'll need to make zippered closures for pillows.

Whether you have an antique treadle machine or the newest computerized model, your sewing machine needs care for peak performance. Cover the machine when not in use. Dust is the enemy. Clean and oil your machine according to the manufacturer's recommendations. With a minimal investment of time, your quilting experience will be trouble-free, and your sewing machine will be your pride and joy.

sewing machine needles

Sewing machine needles are inexpensive and may seem inconsequential, but they are an important item in your sewing toolbox. Have a good supply at the ready. The thread and fabric you're using will determine the size and type of needle you require; consult your sewing machine manual for recommendations.

We find that 80/12 or 75/11 universal needles are good choices for both piecing and quilting. A universal needle has a slightly rounded point and is an all-purpose needle. With sewing machine needles, the larger the number, the thicker the needle shaft. If you experience a needle break when quilting, try a larger needle.

Other options include quilting and Microtex sharp needles. Quilting needles have tapered shafts and are specially engineered to pass through multiple layers. Microtex sharps are tapered with a sharp point and work well for high-thread-count fabrics. Experiment with different needle and thread combinations to find what's best for your quilt and your sewing machine.

Change your machine's needle after every six to eight hours of sewing, and change it immediately if it bends or breaks or if you nick a pin as you sew. Puckering or skipped stitches may mean a dull or bent needle or the wrong size or type of needle.

marking pens and pencils

During both piecing and quilting, you may need to mark on your fabric. Keep a supply of fabric-safe marking tools at hand with choices that will be visible on both light and dark fabrics. We like Clover water-soluble marking pencils for their ease of removal, but we also use chalk markers and a water-soluble pen that we use primarily

for marking quilting lines. A Clover Hera marker, which is not a marker at all but a hard piece of plastic, is also a good choice for marking quilting lines; it works by lightly creasing the fabric, so there are no marks to remove.

seam rippers

You'll know you are an improvisational quilter when you have multiple seam rippers, and you're not afraid to use them. Part of improvising is being able to make changes, and the seam ripper will become your quilting friend.

Seam ripper

pins and binding clips

Pins and pincushions are essential tools in your sewing room. Long flat-head pins work well for piecing. Replace pins when they become dull. Corral those pins with a magnetic pincushion!

If you pin-baste your quilts (as we recommend in chapter 4, page 32), you'll need quilter's safety pins as well. We prefer the No. 3 curved style; they are easiest to open and close. While straight pins can be used to secure binding for handstitching, we prefer binding clips, which look like metal hair clips but are made specifically for securing binding. Both quilter's pins and binding clips are usually available at quilt shops.

design tools

An improvisational approach places you in the role of the designer, and designers need specialized tools. These are the things that will free you to go beyond the pattern and develop your own ideas and concepts.

sketchbooks and pencils

We find it helpful to have several inexpensive notebooks or sketchbooks and a set of markers or colored pencils. Carry a notebook with you and keep one or two in your sewing area. You never know when inspiration will strike, and having a place to record or sketch ideas will prevent those great ideas from being forgotten. A pad of graph paper is also a useful tool for planning quilt designs.

If you're comfortable in the digital world, use your favorite graphic design software to design quilts on your computer. It's an easy way to explore colorways, scale, and other design options with just the click of your mouse.

design wall

A design wall is an integral part of our quiltmaking process. A design wall is essentially a large bulletin board with a flannel cloth surface, useful for placing and working with fabric pieces, quilt blocks, or entire quilt tops. Fabric and blocks will magically stick to the flannel without pins or tape, allowing you to step back and view your work from a distance for better perspective on color, value, and design. See "Make a Design Wall," page 14.

flexible measuring tape

A flexible measuring tape is a must for improvisational quilting. We wear ours around our necks to take quick measurements as we're making blocks or paneling a quilt.

blue painter's tape

Pick up several rolls of blue painter's tape from ¼" (6 mm) to 3" (7.5 cm) wide at the hardware or art supply store. We use this tape to create block and quilt structures on the design wall and for straight-line quilting. Painter's tape is low tack and won't leave residue on your quilts.

materials

Fabric is the quilter's medium. Building a diverse and versatile stash gives you plenty of options when choosing fabrics for your quilts. We like to buy fabric at our local quilt shops because we can see and touch the fabrics before we buy. Online shopping is easy and convenient, though determining the scale of prints and seeing colors accurately can sometimes be difficult. Thread and batting are also essential to quilting, and making the right choices in these materials will help you achieve success.

fabrics and stash building

Our advice for building a great fabric stash: buy the best quality you can afford and buy what you love. From there, think about the versatility of the fabrics you buy.

Solids are basics that you can use for backgrounds, showcasing prints, or on their own. A well-rounded stash has a wide variety of solid fabrics in both neutrals and colors.

Beware of the seductive power of prints and consider scale as you choose them. Those flashy prints may go home with you from the quilt store and never leave your fabric shelf. Small-scale prints are easier to use in patchwork than large-scale prints. Large-scale prints work well as focus fabrics or quilt backings.

Our stashes consist primarily of quilting-weight cottons, but consider other fibers and weaves to add texture to your quilts. Linen, linen and cotton blends, flannel, osnaburg (a cotton utility fabric), and home décor fabrics are all good additions to your stash. Cross-woven fabrics such as shot cottons and chambrays, with warp and weft of different colors, add an interesting dimension to quilts and are great additions to your stash. If you plan to wash your quilt, be sure that all the fabrics you choose are colorfast, washable, and have similar care instructions.

Vintage fabrics have special appeal, but be aware that vintage fabrics may be fragile and may not be colorfast.

Most importantly, build a stash with a wide range of values. A stash isn't built in a day, and we recommend that you buy smartly and slowly. When you see fabrics on sale, ask yourself if you would pay full price for the fabric before you buy. A half-yard (46 cm) cut is a good amount for stash building. Buy more of fabrics that you love and know you will use often. Before you know it, you'll have a colorful, versatile stash from which to choose.

thread

We sew and quilt primarily with 50 weight, 100 percent cotton thread. When choosing thread, remember: the smaller the number, the heavier the thread. Cotton thread is available in a wide range of colors, has high heat tolerance, is strong, and is soft and pliable, which results in flatter seams. Buy quality thread; it's what's holding your quilt together, and cheaper isn't always better.

batting

Batting is the middle layer of a quilt, between the pieced top and the backing. Batting comes in many different fibers and blends, and your choice will affect both the look of the quilting stitches and the final appearance of the quilt.

We use low-loft cotton batting (loft is another word for thickness) in our quilts for several reasons. Cotton is a natural fiber and breathes. Cotton batting shrinks slightly when washed to create the soft, crinkly look we adore. It also resists bearding, or the tendency of small wisps of batting to work their way through the fabric. Low-loft cotton batting is thin, easy to machine quilt, and gives the quilt a slim, antique look when finished.

Polyester, cotton and polyester blend, wool, silk, and bamboo battings are also readily available. Our best advice is to try different fibers and lofts until you find the one that works for you. Read the manufacturer's recommendations on the package to find out how densely the batting must be quilted to remain stable in use and when washed, along with any special instructions for washing and care.

A NOTE ABOUT FABRIC AMOUNTS

We've specified fabric amounts for all of the projects in the book. However, the improvisational nature of these projects makes it impossible to specify yardages exactly. That's especially true of the background and backing fabrics. We've based our yardages on the projects as we made them, but it's always a good idea to buy more. Having more fabric than required provides flexibility and opportunities to try different ideas and back up in case of mistakes. More often than not we purchase more fabric than we might need and save our scraps and use extra fabric or sample blocks to make interesting backs for our quilts.

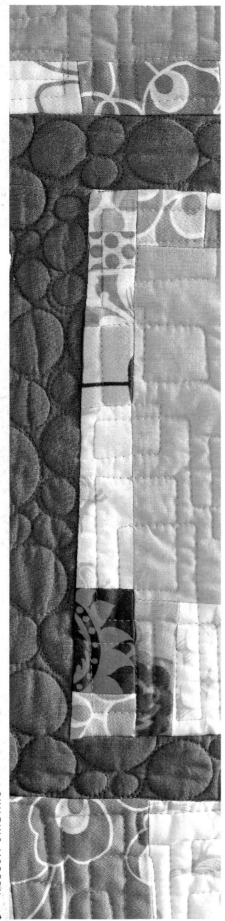

make a design wall

Whether you sew on the kitchen table or have a dedicated studio, there is a design wall option for you. Typically a design wall is a fabric-covered board mounted to the wall, but there are many other options for adding a design wall to your sewing space. You can buy a commercially made design wall, but it is much less expensive to make one of your own that suits your sewing space.

Choose a neutral flannel color, such as white or beige, so colors are not distorted when placed on the surface. If flannel is not available, batting and felt will also work. Place your design wall where you will have at least 6' to 8' (1.8 to 2.5 m) between you and your design wall. Distance is important to be able to get a good perspective on your design and to see differences in value.

flannel-backed tablecloth

A design wall can be as simple as pinning a piece of flannel yardage or batting to a wall; even better, use an inexpensive vinyl or laminate tablecloth with a flannel backing. Add grommets to the tablecloth and a few hooks on the wall, and you'll be able to put it up and take it down as needed. The flannel side is your design wall, and the vinyl or laminate side will allow you to take it down and roll it up with fabric pieces on the flannel until inspiration strikes again.

roller shade for small spaces

If space for a design wall is a challenge, a roller shade in a window or mounted on a door can work as a design wall. Fuse flannel to the shade and pull it down to use when you're working. Roll it up and it disappears.

portable design wall from foam-core board

The following instructions are for a simple design board that you can hang on a wall, lean against a wall, or set on a table. We chose foam-core board because it is inexpensive, readily available at discount or office supply stores, and as a bonus, it is pinnable.

Gather the following materials:

- Foam-core presentation board 20" × 30" (51 × 76 cm)
- ¾ yd (68.5 cm) of 45" (114.5 cm) wide white flannel
- Mailing tape or duct tape
- Picture-hanging nails
- Hammer

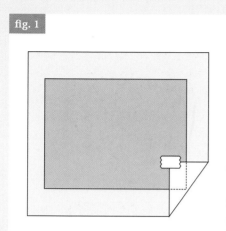

fig. 1

1 | Cut flannel 6" (15 cm) longer and wider than the foam-core board.

2 | Place the flannel right side down on a flat surface. Center the board on top of the flannel. Make sure any markings or labels on the board are facing you so they won't show through the flannel when the board is covered.

3 | Fold the corner of the flannel in as shown in **fig. 1** and secure with a piece of tape. Fold in and tape all four corners.

4 | Fold one side of the flannel smoothly over the edge of the board to the back and secure with a piece of tape at the center. Fold the flannel over the opposite side, pulling the flannel taut, and again secure at the center with a piece of tape. Return to the first edge you taped and pull the flannel smoothly and tautly over the edge of the board, adding pieces of tape between the center and corners until the entire side is secured. Fold and tape the flannel on the opposite side, keeping the flannel taut as you tape.

5 | Repeat Step 4 for the other two sides of the board.

6 | Reinforce the taped edges of the flannel by placing long pieces of tape across each side of the board.

7 | Flip the board over and your design board is complete. Hang using small picture nails.

8 | To make a larger design wall, tape several foam-core boards together. Be sure to tape along the front and back of each joint to stabilize the boards. Cover the joined boards as one, as described above. Alternatively, place individual covered boards side by side to create a larger surface.

sew, what do i need to know?

Our method of improvisational quilting is a mix of precision and a more relaxed approach to cutting and piecing. Basic quilting skills and good habits will serve you well no matter how you choose to approach quilting. The techniques and methods that follow are not absolute rules, but we've found that they work well for us.

preparing fabric

Preparation is one of the keys to successful quilting. You have that shiny new fabric and want to make a quilt—what's next? Prewashing the fabric—or deciding not to—and squaring it up will help you get great results.

to prewash or not to prewash

There are two camps in the quilting community: those who prewash—which means machine washing and drying all fabric before cutting—and those who don't. Katie is the president of the prewash group, while Jacquie only aspires to prewash. Ultimately, it's a personal choice, but let's review the advantages of both sides.

Prewashing removes any chemical residues from the fabric and allows it to shrink before the quilt is made. Fabrics shrink at different rates, and a quilt can sometimes change size dramatically if the fabrics are not prewashed.

Skipping the prewashing step saves time, and the sizing remains in the fabric, giving it a bit more body for handling and cutting.

Whether you prewash or not, iron your fabric before you start cutting. Wrinkly fabric leads to crooked and inaccurate cuts.

Take special care with vintage fabrics. Do prewash or at least test vintage fabrics for any color bleeding or dye migration. It's heartbreaking to wash a finished quilt and have it ruined by bleeding colors.

Whichever option you choose, it's best to apply it to all the fabrics in a quilt; if the entire quilt shrinks, it will retain its beauty better than a quilt in which some areas shrink and others don't. Regard all repurposed scraps from used clothing as preshrunk, and prewash any new fabrics that will be sewn to the recycled pieces.

squaring up

Fabric that's been cut from a bolt may have uneven edges or may be folded off center. Prior to cutting, square up the fabric. With freshly ironed fabric, fold the fabric in half lengthwise, wrong sides together. Line up the two selvedges and adjust the edges until the fold hangs evenly without wrinkles; the cut edges may not align.

Maintaining the even, wrinkle-free fold, lay the fabric on the cutting mat, aligning the fold with a horizontal line on the mat. Use a vertical line on the mat to trim a straight edge **(fig. 1)**. Squaring the fabric ensures that the grain of the fabric is straight and results in straight width-of-fabric cuts with no waviness at the fold.

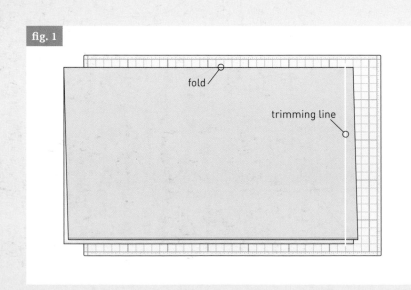

fig. 1

fold

trimming line

cutting

We use a rotary cutter most of the time, but a sharp pair of scissors is a better choice for cutting fabrics to size on the design wall, cutting curved templates accurately, and trimming threads and fabric. We also choose scissors when we want more organically cut edges.

Rotary cutting on a self-healing cutting mat with the aid of a gridded acrylic quilter's ruler is fast, easy, and accurate. Keep a sharp blade in the cutter; dull blades make for jagged cuts. Take special care whenever you're cutting without a ruler as a guide. **Always close the blade of your cutter when not in use.**

To prepare fabric for rotary cutting, square the fabric as described on page 18. Then fold the fabric again, lengthwise, bringing the folded edge into alignment with the selvedges. With a shorter cutting length you don't need to reposition your steadying hand when cutting. Align the ruler with a vertical line on the cutting mat to cut straight strips **(fig. 2)**.

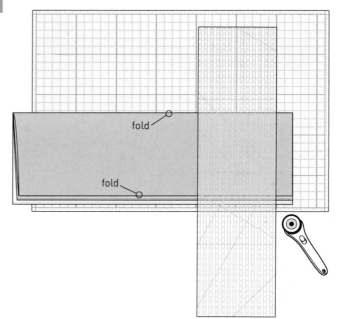

fig. 2

fold

fold

A NOTE ABOUT METRIC CONVERSIONS

We provide metric conversions for all of the instructions in this book. Conversions above 2" (5 cm) are rounded to the nearest half-centimeter.

If your quilt requires precision, please double-check all conversions and adjust if necessary.

We convert ¼" to 6 mm in the text, but please read the section on page 20 on working with scant ¼" seams. To meet this standard, treat 6 mm as a guideline only and keep your seam allowances slightly narrower, about 5 to 5.5 mm.

piecing

Piecing, or joining pieces of fabric together to form a whole, is the heart of patchwork. Making a quilt is a time-consuming labor of love, and with the effort we put into making quilts, we want them to last for a long time. Piecing creates the design, but also forms the underlying structure of the quilt. Learning basic piecing skills will help you create a sturdy, structurally sound quilt that you can love and use for many years.

the scant quarter-inch seam

Quarter-inch (6 mm) seam allowances are the standard in quilt piecing. Accurate piecing will save you a lot of quilting headaches. A ¼" (6 mm) seam in quilting is actually a scant quarter inch, a few threads less than a full ¼" (6 mm); whenever you see "¼" (6 mm) seam allowance" in this book, you'll know it means a scant ¼", or 5.0 to 5.5 mm. The difference is made up by the slight fold or ridge created by the seam and varies with fabric thickness. While it seems like this slight difference wouldn't matter, it can be a problem when it's time to put everything together, and the difference is multiplied across the many seams in a quilt.

Many sewing machines come with a ¼" (6 mm) presser foot attachment that will yield a scant ¼" (6 mm) seam, sometimes called a quilter's foot or piecing foot. Most machines have markings on the throat plate that indicate a ¼" (6 mm) space from the needle. Even with a special foot, it's a good idea to test whether you're sewing an accurate scant ¼" (6 mm), as shown below.

Most of the projects in this book require some precision piecing, so a scant ¼" (6 mm) seam is your friend. In general, accurate ¼" (6 mm) seams are important in improvisational quilting. When joining two or more pieces to measure a certain length, being able to count on a consistent seam allowance makes measuring and construction hassle-free.

THE ¼" (6 MM) SEAM TEST

Cut two 2" × 4" (5 × 10 cm) rectangles. Sew the pieces together along the 4" (10 cm) side using a ¼" (6 mm) seam allowance. Press the seam and measure the unit. It should measure exactly 3½" (9 cm) wide **(fig. 1)**.

If your piece measures more or less, adjust the seam allowance; a 0.5 mm adjustment may be all that's needed. Make adjustments by moving the needle position or by marking a new line to follow on the stitch plate. Some quilters place moleskin or tape on the stitch plates to mark a scant ¼" (6 mm) seam allowance. Repeat the test until you achieve a correct measurement.

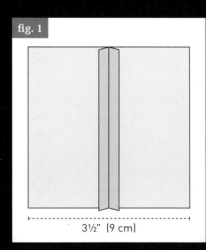

fig. 1

3½" (9 cm)

fig. 1

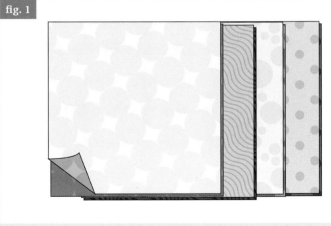

fig. 3

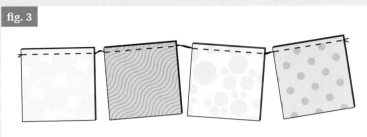

fig. 2

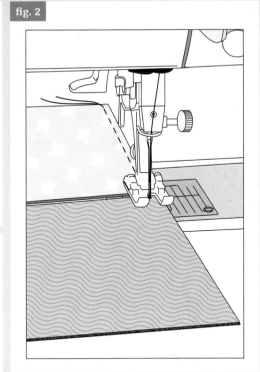

piecing tips

After you've ensured that your presser foot or throat plate marking will yield an accurate scant ¼" (6 mm) seam, you're ready to piece. Use a stitch length of 12 to 15 stitches per inch (2.0 to 1.8 mm) for piecing. If you find that your fabric units are separating at the ends as you handle them, reduce the stitch length. Align fabric edges and sew a nice straight seam. If your edges tend to shift, use a few pins and remove pins as you sew (take it from us, it can be disastrous if the needle hits a pin and breaks). If your edges stay aligned, you can forget the pins.

chain piecing

Chain piecing is a tried-and-true method in traditional quilting, and you can also apply it in improvisational piecing. Chain piecing involves stitching similar units one after the other without clipping the threads between the units. Chain piecing saves time and thread and keeps units in the correct sewing order. Follow these steps for chain piecing.

1 Stack units to be chain pieced with the edge to be sewn to the right. Stack the units beside the sewing machine so they can be picked up in sewing position and moved under the presser foot in an orderly manner. Stacking in this way ensures that the correct side is sewn **(fig. 1)**.

2 Stitch the seam of the first unit and stop with the needle down at the end of the unit. Without lifting the presser foot or clipping the threads, feed the second unit under the presser foot **(fig. 2)**.

3 Continue feeding and sewing all of the units in order. Clip the final threads after sewing the last unit, and the units will be connected in a long chain that you can carry to the ironing board for pressing **(fig. 3)**.

4 Clip the threads between the units and press seam allowances open or to the side (as described in the following section), stacking the units in order after pressing.

pressing

Don't you love it when seams lie flat and a block is crisp and square? Pressing uses the weight of the iron and its heat to remove wrinkles and flatten seams by lifting the iron up and down. Ironing is moving the iron back and forth. Pressing is for quilters!

seam allowance direction

Some quilters press seam allowances to the side, and some press seam allowances open. Pressing to the side has been the standard for many years, but pressing open is gaining in popularity. We press open the majority of the time, but it depends on the block, the technique, and the quilt. We prefer pressing open because the seams lie flat. The projects in this book include directions for pressing seam allowances.

steam pressing

Using the steam function of your iron is also a matter of preference. Be aware that steam may distort sewn units, especially if you use an ironing motion—avoid this. Steam can be very effective if you use it to properly press seam intersections.

rogue pressing

You can use pressing to create crooked or wavy seams, giving blocks a free-sewn look. Throw out the rules of conventional pressing. To achieve a wavy seam look, press the seam allowances to the side using a back-and-forth ironing motion and lots of steam. The steam and the pull of the iron will skew the seam out of alignment and create a wavy look.

OUR BASIC PRESSING METHOD

1 | "Set" the seam before pressing it. Place the sewn unit flat on the ironing board as sewn (wrong side up). Lower the iron onto the fabric for a few seconds to set the seam and merge threads and fabric.

2 | Press the seam. Open the sewn unit and place it wrong side up. Finger press to open the seam. Press the seam flat, lifting and lowering the iron rather than sliding back and forth. For long seams, use the tip of the iron to open the seam, press, open more seam, press, and continue the length of the seam.

3 | Flip the sewn unit right side up and press again from the right side. A couple of final touches with the iron will result in a nice flat seam.

a good match

Most quilts require joining units and matching seams. It's not difficult to get good results; just go slowly until you're comfortable with the process. We tend to use a pin or two when joining, especially if a perfect match is the goal. That said, try not to focus on perfection—it can be paralyzing. If your seams are a smidge off from a perfect match here and there, it won't affect the beauty or utility of the quilt. Small imperfections disappear and the beauty emerges.

match units with seam allowances pressed to the side

When joining units with seam allowances pressed to the side, seams will nest together when they are lying in opposite directions. Pressing to the side creates a tiny ridge. Nesting seams takes advantage of those ridges by butting them against each other **(fig. 1)**.

Pin the side of the seam allowance that the needle will reach last. This pin keeps the intersection of the seams from shifting and allows you to sew up to the seam, remove the pin, and continue sewing. With seam allowances pressed to the side, be aware of which direction the seams are pressed as you assemble your quilt so that nesting is possible.

match units with seam allowances pressed open

To match units with seam allowances pressed open, align the seams directly on top of each other, right sides together. Some quilters stab a pin through the center of the top and bottom seams to align. We simply wiggle them together between our fingers to match the seams **(fig. 2)**.

When joining sections of a quilt that contain multiple seams to match, pin at each intersecting seam and every 4" to 6" (10 to 15 cm) along the seam.

These basics for preparation, cutting, piecing, and pressing are the foundation of quiltmaking and will help you make quilts that are both beautiful and well crafted.

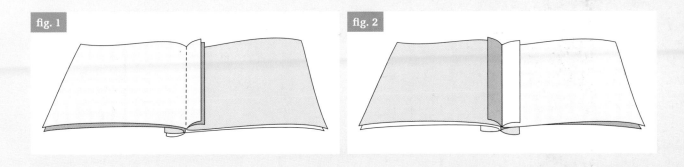

fig. 1

fig. 2

COLOR AND DESIGN

beyond the crayon box

How do we decide on a color story and choose the fabrics for a quilt? Sometimes a fabric is the starting point for a quilt; that fabric establishes the color scheme, and we go from there. For other quilts we have a color or a color scheme in mind and choose fabrics to fit the scheme. Sometimes the quilt design leads us to the color and fabric choices. We rely on instinct and intuition to choose colors and fabrics, and as we've learned about color, value, and design, our process has become more thoughtful and deliberate. As you choose your own fabrics for quilts, don't be timid. If you make a mistake, learn from it. What's the worst that can happen? You might need to make another fabric purchase!

what's in the crayon box?

Translating color ideas to fabric and then to a quilt requires planning and thought. We like to think of it as going beyond the crayon box.

The color wheel is filled with gorgeous colors to choose from. Buy a color wheel or make one to keep in your sewing space. A color wheel is inspirational and a good resource as you learn to choose and combine colors.

You know the colors you like, but how can you make them work for you in a quilt? Knowing a little about color theory might help you better understand the color choices you make and expand your color choices.

Three basic color schemes are monochromatic, complementary, and analogous colors. We think of them this way:

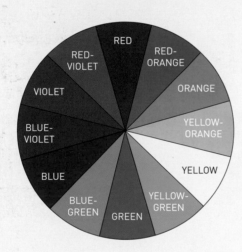

Keep a color wheel in your sewing room.

✳ A **monochromatic** color scheme is tints, shades, and tones of the same color **(fig. 1)**. Picture members of the same family dressed in lighter and darker clothes of the same hue. Monochromatic quilts can be soothing or moody and dramatic. Be careful, though, as monochromatic can be monotonous and boring, too.

✳ **Complementary** colors are opposite each other on the color wheel. Blue and orange, red and green, and violet and yellow are examples of complements **(fig. 2)**. These color combinations are naturally dynamic. Complements are inherently high contrast and create excitement and dramatic impact in a quilt. They can also be harsh. You can tone down complements by using less-saturated versions of each color.

✳ **Analogous** colors live next to each other on the color wheel. Blue, blue-green, and green or red, red-orange, and orange are examples of analogous colors **(fig. 3)**. They're neighbors, so they get along well together and create a harmonious look. Consider proportion when using an analogous color scheme. Analogous colors work best when one color is the star of the show, and the others are supporting players.

Print fabrics are trickier to work with than solid swatches of color. The fabrics on page 27 are our interpretations of the three basic color schemes in prints.

fig. 1 *Monochromatic colors*

fig. 2 *Complementary colors*

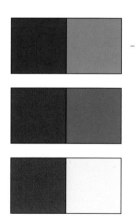

fig. 3 *Analogous colors*

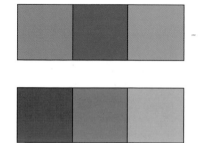

beyond the crayon box

Choosing fabrics is about value as much as it is about color. Value is the lightness or darkness of a color—the simplest classification is light, medium, and dark. Value differences create contrast and define lines and shapes within a quilt design. Using value to raise or lower contrast can change the mood of a quilt; intentional placement of values draws the eye to certain parts of the quilt or moves the eye across the quilt. Value is a powerful design tool.

Notice in **fig.1** how the design is more defined in the square on the right. The value difference defines the shape.

Value is relative. A fabric can be a medium in one situation and a dark or a light in another depending on what value sits next to it. To see value, place fabrics on your design wall and stand back as far as you can to see how the fabrics relate to each other. Sometimes it helps to squint your eyes a bit. Use a digital camera when you begin to explore value; take a picture of your fabrics and convert it to black and white to remove the color and see the values. You might be surprised by what you see.

Large-scale prints are value tricksters. Different sections of a fabric can register different values. Most fabrics in quilt shops are medium in value, so look specifically for lights and darks when you shop.

Distinguishing different values is easier with fabrics of similar color, such as a group of reds. Combining colors is more challenging, but remember it's not about a right answer; it's about putting fabrics together that enhance your design.

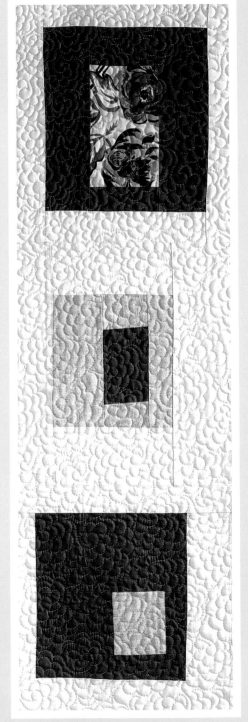

fig. 1

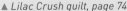
▲ *Lilac Crush quilt, page 74*

use what you know

Think about the quilt you want to make and how different values might make the design shine. Dark-value fabrics placed next to light-value fabrics create the most contrast. If you want crisply defined shapes in your design, use these values together.

A high concentration of medium values in a design softens the edges of shapes and results in a more blended, flowing look. Designs don't have to have high contrast to be effective. Too little contrast may, however, result in muddy-looking blocks or quilts.

Observing completed quilts in this book will help you learn more about the power of value. For example, while contrasting colors clearly define the rings in the Supernova quilt on page 104, the light and dark values within the plum and mustard rings create movement and interest within each ring. The radiating value differences support the overall design of the quilt. High contrast and complementary colors combine to create a bold, dynamic design.

The design of the Illusions quilt on page 170 depends heavily on value. The darker fabric against the light yellow creates contrast, defining the forms of the pods and producing the illusion of circles. The careful placement of different values in the diamond shapes creates a secondary design.

The Stepping-Stones quilt, page 132, and the Mod TV quilt, page 70, have similar analogous color schemes, but Mod TV's blocks are more defined due to the higher contrast between the blocks and the background. The blocks in the Stepping-Stones quilt blend more with the background and the quilt has a soft, quiet feel. On page 30, you'll see the value relationships in these four quilts at a glance.

Making fabric choices takes time. Cut fabric swatches and place them on the design wall. Add and take away. Leave the swatches up for a few days so you can come back to them often. Make a sample block to test fabrics before you dive into a whole quilt. Let your instinct be your guide, along with a little knowledge of color and value.

▲ Contrasting values give the Illusions quilt impact and complexity.

▲ Light and dark values create movement in the Supernova quilt.

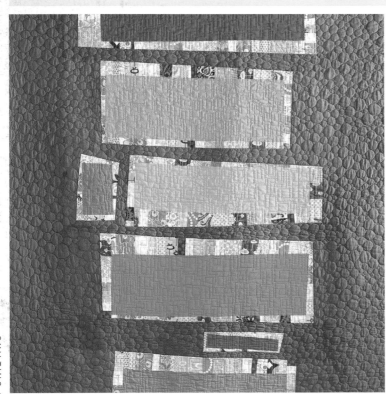

▲ The Stepping-Stones quilt has an analogous color scheme.

▲ The Mod TV quilt uses analogous colors with high contrast between blocks and background.

put it all together

Neither of us is trained in art or design; Jacquie's C-minus in drawing in college is evidence of that. Nor has our lack of formal training discouraged us from diving into the design process full force. We started small, moving away from using just one fabric line in our quilts, then went on to manipulating other people's designs, to finally creating our own. Design is an exhilarating process, and we've learned through experience. Here are a few basics to pique your interest and encourage you to learn more on your own.

design elements

Think of your quilt as a composition. Whether you know it or not, as you make a quilt you are using the elements and principles of design. Elements of design are the "what" in your quilt, the things we see. They include:

* **Color.** You know this one. You have countless exciting choices!

* **Value.** Value is the degree of lightness or darkness in a design, and as noted, value is an important consideration for quilts.

* **Shape.** Shapes can be geometric, such as circles, squares, and rectangles, or organic and free-form. Quilters often use squares, rectangles, and triangles, but these are only a starting point.

* **Size.** Shapes in your quilt can be large or small, and their relationship to each other and to the overall quilt size is important to the design.

* **Texture.** Texture is roughness or smoothness and can be real or visual. Create texture in your quilt through the fabrics you choose and with the quilting itself.

* **Space.** Space is all that blank area around the shapes in your quilt. Some designs have lots of space, and some have very little. The space around the blocks or surrounding the shapes in a quilt is another design opportunity.

* **Line.** Lines are marks that form outlines and define shapes. We use the element of line in both the piecing and the quilting of a project.

Most quilts will emphasize one or more of these design elements. Great design lies in how the elements are combined.

basics of composition

If the design elements we've listed are the *what,* then the principles of putting the elements together in a pleasing composition are the *how.* We think of these principles as guides, good ideas to consider as you design, rather than hard and fast rules.

* **Contrast.** Contrast is directly related to value and color; it highlights the differences in the design.

* **Emphasis.** Emphasis is about importance. Where do you want viewers to look first when they see your quilt? Emphasis can be created by color, value, size, or placement.

* **Balance.** Balance is about creating equal visual weight in a design. It can be achieved through symmetry or asymmetry. Unbalanced designs can also be intriguing.

* **Unity.** A unified design feels like it fits together. Repetition of similar shapes can unify a design. Color can also be a unifying element.

* **Pattern.** Quilts are all about pattern and repetition. Modern quilts may have less pattern and repetition than traditional quilts.

* **Movement.** Movement is the suggestion of motion in a quilt.

* **Rhythm.** Rhythm in design is like rhythm in music. A design with rhythm has a sense of flow. If a design feels static and motionless, introduce some new elements to build rhythm.

All those technical terms can be intimidating and confusing, but they don't have to be. You won't learn about design by reading about it. Skill with design comes from working with fabric, color, and shapes. Sounds like making a quilt, doesn't it? So make a quilt and keep this information in the back of your mind. Make a conscious effort to notice and recognize when the elements and principles come into play as you make a quilt. Enjoy the process and learn more with each quilt you make.

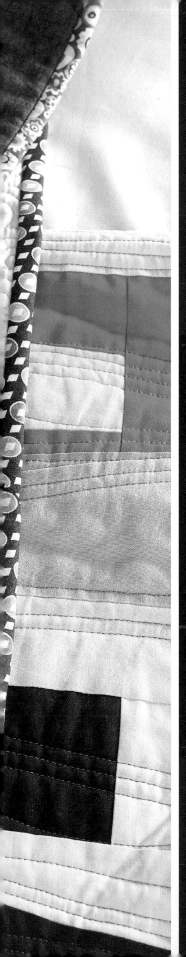

finishing touches

BACKING, QUILTING, BINDING, AND MORE

You've completed your quilt top, and it's time to turn it into a finished quilt. Along with tips for basic steps such as preparing the quilt top and basting the quilt sandwich, here are our best tips, advice, and instructions for making final design decisions about quilting and binding. We also include instructions in this chapter for adding an invisible zipper to quilted pillow projects. If you're a beginner, just take your time and go step by step. If you're a more experienced quilter, use your own favorite methods or try ours. As you finish one modern improvisational quilt, you're sure to find yourself planning the next one.

prepare the quilt sandwich

Carefully preparing the quilt top and quilt sandwich will make your quilting and binding easier and will help you get high-quality results. Be sure that you have a clean, flat workspace that's large enough to accommodate your entire quilt and that's comfortable for you to work in.

staystitching

Have you experienced seams in your quilt top coming apart at the outer edges of the quilt? It's easy for pieced fabric to separate at the seams, especially if you handle the quilt top a lot before quilting. Staystitching prevents this problem.

Staystitching is a single line of stitching through one layer of fabric. It stabilizes the fabric and prevents stretching. Using a normal or slightly shorter stitch length, staystitch around the perimeter of the top before you assemble the quilt sandwich. Stitch slightly less than ¼" (6 mm)

from the edge so the staystitching doesn't show after the binding is attached **(fig. 1)**.

After staystitching, trim any stray threads on the wrong side of the quilt top. Press the quilt top and the backing to prepare for basting. The quilt backing and batting should be at least 4" (10 cm) larger than the top on all sides. Be sure the batting is free from wrinkles or folds.

basting the sandwich

Basting holds the backing, batting, and quilt top—the three layers of a quilt—together and prevents the layers from shifting during quilting. There are several methods for basting a quilt, but we prefer pin basting. We use size 3 (2" [5 cm]) curved safety pins, made especially for quilting and available at fabric and quilting shops, because we find them easiest to open and close. Other methods include quilt basting spray, a temporary adhesive designed to

hold the layers together without shifting, and basting by hand with a needle and thread, making long stitches across the quilt sandwich. We don't recommend basting by hand if you're planning to quilt by machine.

Gather the quilt top, batting, backing, painter's tape, and quilter's curved safety pins. Follow these easy steps.

1   Place the quilt backing wrong side up on a flat surface such as a floor or table. Tape all four edges of the quilt backing to the surface with painter's tape so that the back is taut, but not stretched, and free of wrinkles.

2   Layer the batting over the backing and smooth the batting outward from the center so there are no wrinkles or folds. Be careful not to stretch the batting.

3   Center the quilt top, right side up, over the batting. Smooth the top from the center to the edges so it is flat and wrinkle-free. This is what we refer to as the quilt sandwich of backing, batting, and quilt top. The backing and batting should extend beyond the quilt top on all sides by several inches.

4   Start at the center of the quilt top and place pins every 3" to 4" (7.5 to 10 cm). Work from the center to the edges until the entire top is pinned.

5   Remove the tape. With basting complete, the project is ready for quilting.

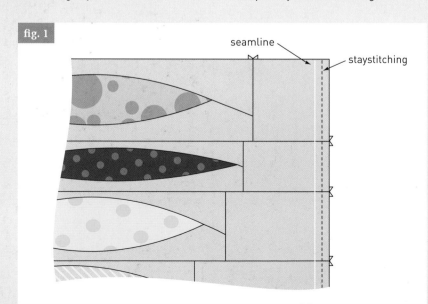

fig. 1

seamline

staystitching

make a pieced backing

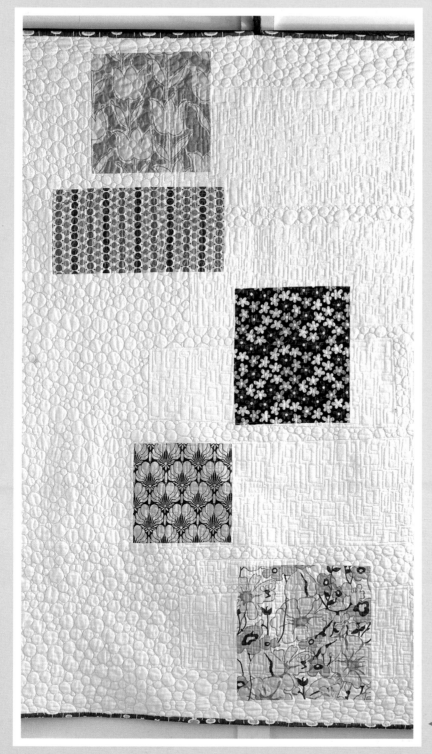

We've used pieced backings on many of the quilts in this book. A pieced backing serves many purposes: it widens the backing fabric so you can buy less of a single fabric; it gives you an opportunity to use bits and pieces of fabric left over from making the quilt top; it can make use of an extra block or two; it can even make the quilt reversible.

A pieced backing is most economical when you need a backing fabric that is just a little larger than the fabric width. Split the backing fabric lengthwise (along the center or to one side) and insert a panel of piecing between the two halves to bring the backing width to the necessary measurement. Be sure the decorative addition to the backing won't be trimmed away as the quilt is squared after quilting.

You can piece the quilt back as if it were a separate improvisational quilt. Add fabric to make the backing piecework at least 4" (10 cm) larger on all sides than the quilt top and proceed as usual with finishing the quilt.

◄ *Pieced backing on Stepping-Stones quilt, page 132*

quilt as desired

The quilts in this book were all quilted by machine, either on a home machine or on a long-arm quilting machine. Perhaps you've read the phrase, "quilt as desired" and asked yourself, *how do I know what I desire?* It can be daunting to think about how to quilt your quilt. And all too often, we see a beautiful quilt top that's been quilted without regard for its design.

Follow our suggestions to make your decision and use quilting to enhance the quilt design. Take both your skill level and the design of the quilt into consideration as you make your quilting decisions. Design options include:

* **Stitch in the Ditch.** To stitch in the ditch means to quilt along the seamlines of the quilt top. We don't recommend stitching in the ditch except as a way to provide stability to sections of the quilt before additional quilting is added. Stitch in the ditch adds little in terms of enhancing the design.

* **Overall Design.** Overall designs such as meandering (**fig. 7, page 38**) and straight-line

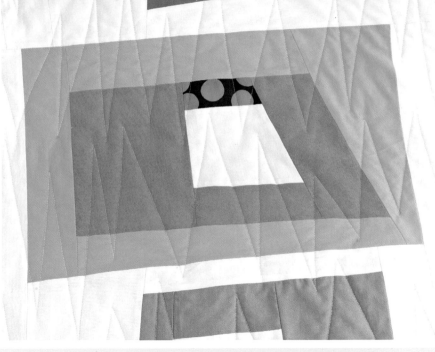

▲ *Mod TV quilt, page 70*

A walking foot attachment for your sewing machine is essential for straight-line quilting.

quilting (**figs. 1, 2, 3, and 4, page 37**) provide unity, create texture, and showcase the quilt design as a whole. Think about how the overall quilting design will complement the feeling you want to achieve in the finished quilt. Do you want to add softness to the design with the flowing lines of a meander, or emphasize the triangles in a quilt with a diamond crosshatch? The Fractured quilt on page 126 is an example of how a simple overall quilting pattern emphasizes the quilt design. Random lines create a fractured look that mimics the fractured design in the piecing.

* **Highlight the Piecing.** Use different kinds of quilting in different areas of the quilt to highlight the piecing and bring emphasis to parts of the quilt. Quilting different designs in the blocks and the background can define background areas and shapes and provide emphasis in pieced areas. The Shattered

quilt on page 92 has quilting that draws attention to the shapes formed by the piecing.

* **Fit the Theme.** Think about the inspiration or theme of the quilt and design the quilting to fit the theme. The serpentine stitch on the Urban Garden quilt on page 52 reminded us of plowed furrows, and the zigzag quilting of the Mod TV quilt on page 70 looks like static-filled television screens. Quilting that fits the theme of a quilt can add whimsy and accentuates the design. On the Supernova quilt, page 104, the quilting emphasizes the explosive feeling of the design, beginning in the center and expanding outward to tiny pebbles at the edges.

Some quilters like to photograph the finished quilt top, print several large copies of the image, and then use marking pens to try different quilt patterns on the images. This method gives you immediate visual feedback on the success of a quilting pattern with the quilt top.

quilting on a home sewing machine

Most home sewing machines today are equipped for both machine-fed quilting in straight lines with a walking foot and for free-motion quilting, a technique for "drawing" with the needle while the machine's feed dog mechanism is lowered or covered. A sewing machine with a walking foot attachment and the ability to lower the feed dog gives you myriad quilting options.

straight-line quilting

A walking foot attachment for your machine is essential for straight-line quilting. Also called an even-feed foot, the walking foot acts as an additional feed dog on top of the fabric, feeding the layers of the quilt sandwich through the machine without shifting. Straight lines are easy to accomplish and the design potential is unlimited.

Try different line spacing and combinations of lines to create interesting quilting patterns; intersecting lines create additional shapes on the quilt such as squares, rectangles, and diamonds. Plot the quilting lines at regular intervals or randomly. Straight-line quilting, with its linear, clean feel, is especially appropriate for modern quilts **(figs. 1, 2, 3, and 4)**.

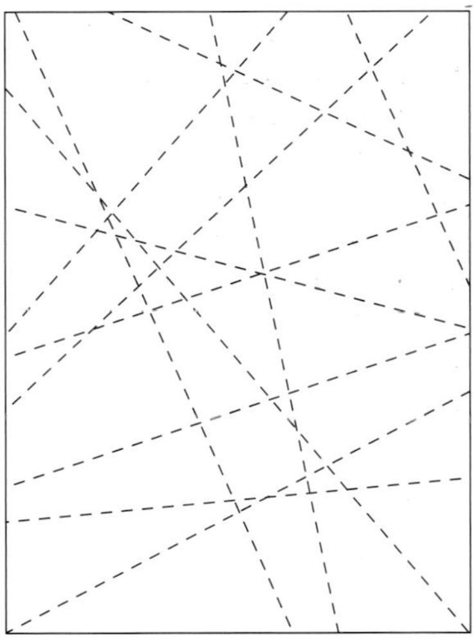

To begin straight-line quilting, establish an initial line using painter's tape on the quilt top. Painter's tape is low-tack and will not leave a residue on the quilt. Place the initial line across the center of the quilt if possible. Follow the edge of the tape with

fig. 1 *Double Crosshatch*

fig. 2 *Combination*

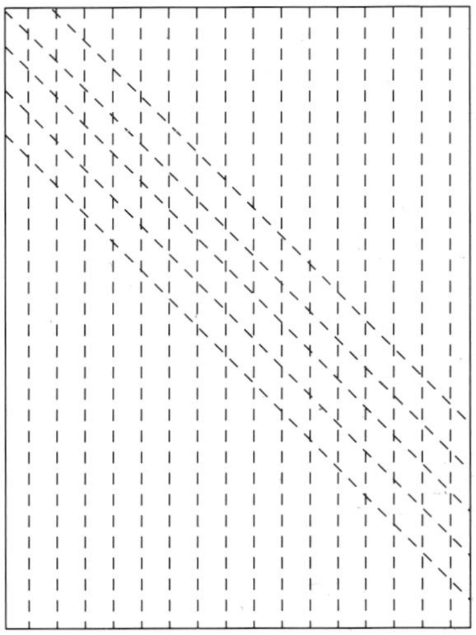

fig. 3 *Graduated Lines*

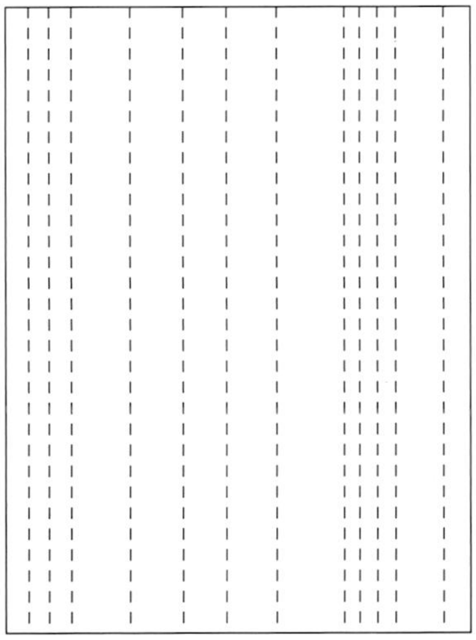

fig. 4 *Fracture Quilting*

the edge of the walking foot to quilt a straight line. Make subsequent lines using the walking foot edge as a guide, or move the tape to quilt the next line.

Quilt lines from the center outward, working first with one side of the quilt and then the other by rotating the quilt sandwich. As an alternative to tape, mark lines with a fabric-safe marker; test on a scrap first to ensure removability. Sew directly on the marked lines to quilt the quilt.

quilting gentle curves

You can use a home sewing machine with a walking foot attachment to quilt gentle curves (**fig. 5**) or organic line quilting such as that in **fig. 6**. Use gentle curves to fill areas on your quilt; they'll create additional curved shapes between the lines. To create organic line quilting, stitch subtle wavy lines across the quilt, beginning near the center of the quilt and spacing the lines from ¼" to 1" (6 mm to 2.5 cm) apart. Guide the quilt layers to gently wave and flow while quilting the lines. Mark the lines before sewing or quilt the curves freehand.

free-motion quilting

Free-motion quilting requires a sewing machine with a feed dog that can be lowered or covered and a darning foot. Free-motion quilting is a bit like drawing with thread. To free-motion quilt, the quilter moves the quilt as the machine stitches to create the quilting design. You are in control of both the design and the stitch length.

Free-motion quilting takes practice. The aim is to create even stitch lengths and stitch in a smooth rhythm. Mastering a new skill takes many hours of practice, and free-motion quilting is no exception. Practice on sample pieces or small projects and quilts.

Free-motion quilting is a bit more challenging than quilting with a walking foot, but many quilters love to quilt this way. We recommend

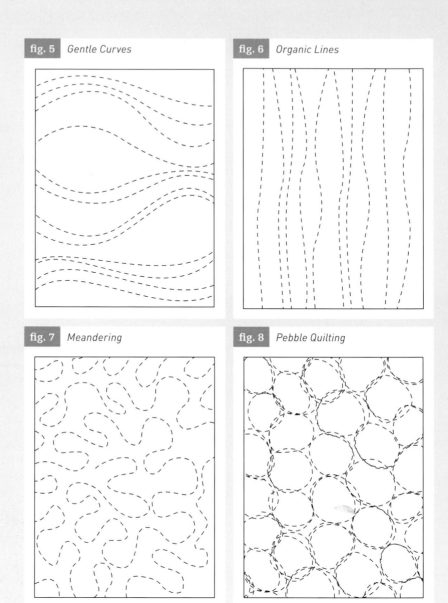

fig. 5 *Gentle Curves*

fig. 6 *Organic Lines*

fig. 7 *Meandering*

fig. 8 *Pebble Quilting*

taking a free-motion class from your local quilt shop, working with a friend, or if you like to learn on your own, see the recommended reading on page 174. Take the plunge and give it a try.

There are a few tools that, while not essential, we've found helpful when free-motion quilting. Quilting gloves with rubber-tipped fingers are available in most quilting and fabric stores; these help you grip the quilt and move it smoothly under the needle. We've also found that using a slick mat that fits under the needle and covers part of the sewing machine table (we like the Supreme Slider brand) can reduce friction and allow the quilt to move more easily.

quilting on a long-arm machine

Meandering and pebble quilting **(figs. 7 and 8)** are two common free-motion designs. If you're a beginner, try free-form designs like these to get the feel of free-motion quilting.

decorative stitches

Many sewing machines can create decorative stitches. The serpentine stitch that we used on the Urban Garden quilt on page 52 is one example. Many machines also have a scallop stitch and almost all have a zigzag stitch. Check your sewing machine manual for the stitches available on your machine and their compatibility with a walking foot.

Long-arm quilting machines allow the operator to quilt a full-size quilt in just a few hours. Some quilt shops have long-arm machines that you can learn to use and rent by the hour, or you can send the quilt to be quilted to your specifications by a long-arm machine operator for a fee.

We enjoy collaborating with Angela Walters, a long-arm quilter in Kansas City, Missouri, who artfully executed the more complex quilting designs in the book. While we love quilting our own quilts, a long-arm machine provides more options for quilting than a home sewing machine and can save a lot of time.

Choose your long-arm operator carefully. Ask to see samples

of work and have a face-to-face discussion to talk about quilting philosophy and possible designs. Help your long-arm quilter understand your design aesthetic and share your likes and dislikes. If he or she specializes in feather shapes and wants to fill your quilt with them, and feathers aren't your thing, find another quilter.

Don't turn your quilt over to your long-arm stitcher with carte blanche. It's your quilt and he or she should make suggestions for quilting but listen to your ideas as well. We worked with Angela in part because her goal is not to showcase her quilting, but to use her quilting skills to enhance our piecing.

The following projects were quilted by Angela Walters on a long-arm machine:

- Sea Glass quilt, page 56
- Lilac Crush quilt, page 74
- Add It Up quilt, page 88
- Shattered quilt, page 92
- Supernova quilt, page 104
- Stepping-Stones quilt, page 132
- Winter Windows quilt, page 140
- Illusions quilt, page 170

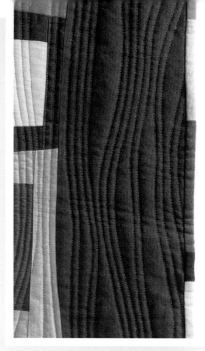

square and bind the quilt

After the quilt sandwich is quilted, just a few steps remain. Binding the quilt offers another opportunity to choose color and design. Prepare to apply the binding by squaring the quilt.

squaring

Squaring the quilt after quilting and before binding ensures straight edges and 90-degree corners; even the most meticulously pieced quilt can go out of square after quilting. To square a quilt, use a 6" × 24" (15 × 61 cm) acrylic quilter's ruler and a rotary cutter and follow these steps:

1   Start in one corner of the quilt. Place the short end of the ruler along the bottom edge of the quilt and align the long side with the perpendicular edge of the quilt **(fig. 1)**.

2   If the quilt waves inside or outside of the ruler's edge, gently ease the quilt by pulling on the excess backing and batting or on the inside of the quilt to straighten the edge. But remember that extremely wavy sides may be a result of improvisational piecing and quilting, and some fabric may need to be trimmed during the process of squaring. If the quilt has borders, it may be more effective to align the ruler with straight seams inside the quilt top, trimming the quilt edge parallel with the seams.

3   When the edge of the quilt is aligned along the 24" (61 cm) side of the ruler, hold the ruler steady and use a rotary cutter to trim the excess batting and backing fabric.

4   Continue this process around the quilt. Try not to tug when easing the quilt; pull gently. The quilt is pliable and will move back into square.

Binding on Tipsy City quilt, page 164 ▲

fig. 1

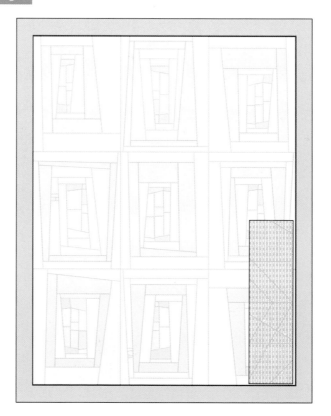

binding

Binding encloses and protects the edges of the quilt. Choosing the fabric for the quilt binding is the final design decision and an opportunity to enhance your design. Seize it. Take time to consider options. We're always surprised by the visual impact that ¼" (6 mm) of binding fabric makes.

We rarely choose the binding fabric until the quilt top is complete, and we audition several fabric options before cutting the strips. Place fabrics under the quilt so only ¼" (6 mm) of the fabric is revealed. Stand back and consider each choice.

Binding can add a color that doesn't appear in the quilt top, or it can emphasize a color that does appear. Binding can add whimsy to a serious quilt or calm a busy quilt. Binding can disappear so that the pieced design is the one and only focus or add a dramatic frame

that encloses a design and draws attention to it. Pieced binding can add another dimension—a small pieced section of binding may be that perfect finishing detail. The Tipsy City quilt on page 164 (and at left), is a good example of this.

With the binding fabric chosen, you're ready to transform the top into a quilt. Follow these steps.

1   Gather your quilt with all quilting completed, a 6" × 24" (15 × 61 cm) acrylic quilter's ruler, fabric for binding, and thread to match binding. You'll also need binding clips, pins, small scissors or thread snips, a handsewing needle, and of course, your sewing machine. Your walking foot attachment is optional.

2   Cut 2¼" (5.5 cm) wide strips of binding fabric on the straight crosswise grain. To calculate the amount of binding needed

for a quilt, when working with 45" (114.5 cm) wide fabric, measure the perimeter of the quilt by adding the lengths of the four sides. Add an additional 20" (51 cm) for the mitered corners and tails for joining the final seam. Divide the total number by 40 (if in inches) or by 102 (if in centimeters) and round up.

3   For example, for a 50" × 50" quilt:

✳ 50" + 50" + 50" + 50" = 200"

✳ 200" + 20" = 220" of binding

✳ 220" divided by 40 = 5.5, rounded up to 6 strips. Six strips 2¼" wide by the full width of the fabric are needed to bind this quilt.

4   Remove the selvedges and join the binding strips with diagonal seams to create a continuous strip of binding. Place the strips as shown in **fig. 1**, right sides together, and sew on the diagonal from corner to corner. Trim the excess fabric above the stitching line leaving a ¼" (6 mm) seam allowance. Repeat this process to join all of your binding strips.

5   Press seams open and trim the triangles that extend past the top and bottom of the strip so the strip looks like **fig. 2**.

6   Fold the binding strip in half lengthwise, wrong sides together, and press.

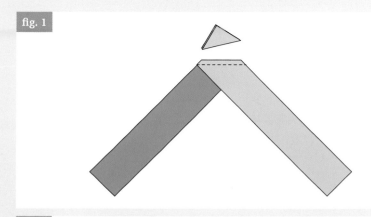

fig. 1

fig. 2

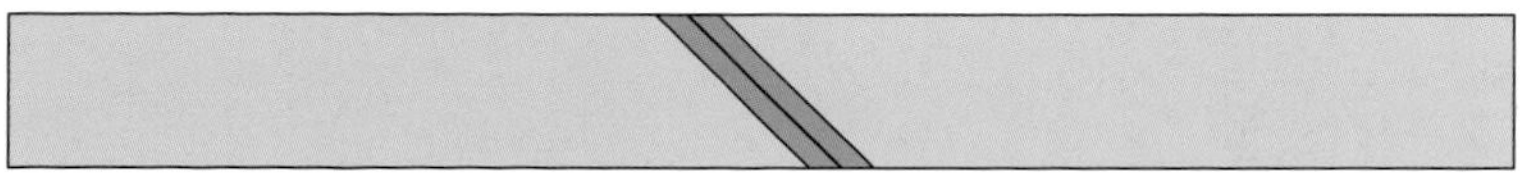

7 Attach the walking foot, a ¼" (6 mm) piecing foot, or an all-purpose presser foot to the sewing machine. Align the binding's raw edges with one edge of the quilt top, right sides together. Leave an 8" to 10" (20.5 to 25.5 cm) tail of binding free at the start and begin sewing at the point shown in **fig. 3**, about two-thirds of the way along one edge of the quilt. Backstitch to secure and continue sewing using a ¼" (6 mm) seam.

8 Stop sewing ¼" (6 mm) from the corner. Backstitch, cut the threads, and remove the quilt from beneath the presser foot **(fig. 4)**.

9 Rotate the quilt into position for stitching the next edge. To create a mitered corner, fold the binding upward from the last stitch at a 45-degree angle **(fig. 5)**.

10 Keeping the original fold in place, fold the binding forward so it extends along the next

side of the quilt. Pin the resulting pleat at the corner. Start sewing at the top edge, backstitching to secure, and continue sewing to ¼" (6 mm) from the next corner. Repeat the mitering process for the other three corners.

11 After mitering the last corner, sew to a point about 10" to 15" (25.5 to 38 cm) from the starting point **(fig. 6)**. Backstitch and cut the threads. Trim the excess binding, leaving a tail about

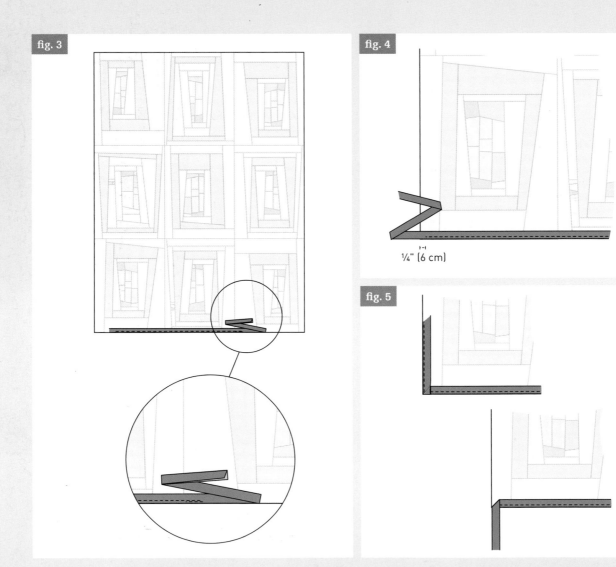

fig. 3

fig. 4

¼" (6 cm)

fig. 5

10" (25.5 cm) long. In the following text, B indicates the beginning tail of binding, and E indicates the ending tail.

12 To join the ends and complete the binding, extend end B along the quilt edge and cut the tail so it ends at the center of the gap. Extend end E along the quilt edge and fold it back on itself where it meets B. Finger press the fold **(fig. 7)**.

13 Measure 2¼" (5.5 cm) from the fold, toward end E, and make a mark on the binding. Unfold the strip and cut straight across E at the mark **(fig. 8)**.

14 Completely unfold the strip ends and place them right sides together at a right angle. Pin the ends together on the diagonal and refold the binding before sewing to ensure neither end is twisted. Sew on the diagonal and trim, leaving a ¼" (6 mm) seam allowance **(fig. 9)**.

15 Finger press the seam open and refold the binding. Align the joined binding with the quilt edge and sew across the gap.

16 Wrap the binding to the back of the quilt and secure with binding clips or pins. The binding's folded edge should just cover the stitching line.

17 Stitch the binding's folded edge to the back of the quilt using a ladder stitch (our preference) or slip stitch. Stitch the miters closed as you stitch around the quilt.

fig. 6

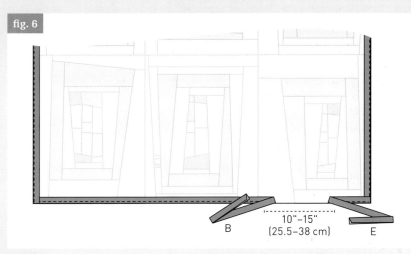

B   10"–15"   E
(25.5–38 cm)

fig. 7

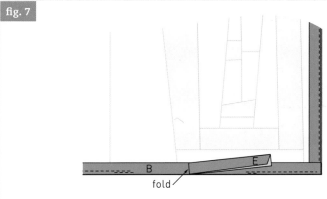

B   E
fold

fig. 8

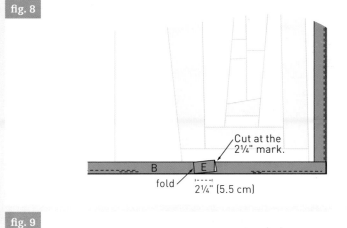

Cut at the 2¼" mark.

B   E

fold
2¼" (5.5 cm)

fig. 9

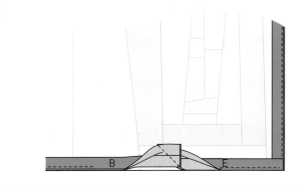

B   E

invisible-zipper closure for pillows

We made the pillows in this book with backs that have an invisible zipper for a clean, modern, professional finish. It's not hard to do this with a sewing machine and regular zipper foot. Follow these steps for best results.

Note: Invisible zippers are available in a limited number of sizes, but they are easy to shorten. Measure the zipper from the top stops to the desired length and mark. Zigzag across the zipper teeth (a plastic coil) to create a new bottom stop and cut away the excess zipper.

1 Gather the pillow top, fabric for pillow back, pillow form, and invisible zipper. You'll need pins, a hem gauge, and a point turner or knitting needle for smoothing corners, as well as your sewing machine with zipper foot and walking foot attachments. A special invisible zipper foot is optional.

2 Be sure the pillow top and pillow back are square and 1" (2.5 cm) larger in all dimensions than the pillow form.

3 Unzip the invisible zipper and place it wrong side up on the ironing board. Uncurl the teeth on the zipper tape by ironing them at a low heat setting so the teeth of the zipper lie to the front of the zipper tape and the back is flat. Be careful not to melt the polyester zipper; use a press cloth if necessary.

4 Lay the opened zipper along the bottom edge of the pillow top, right sides together, with the outer edge of the zipper tape **(side A, fig. 1)** along the pillow's raw edge and the entire zipper on the pillow.

5 Center the zipper from side to side on the pillow top. Measure from the bottom of the zipper teeth to the pillow edge (C) and from the top of the zipper teeth to the opposite edge (D) and confirm that the measurement is the same. Record this measurement to use later.

6 Pin Side A of the zipper tape to the bottom edge of the pillow. Place another pin at the top of the zipper to mark where the zipper teeth begin.

7 Install the zipper foot on your machine and adjust the needle position so that the stitching line will be about 1/16" (1.5 mm) from the zipper teeth. *Note:* If you prefer to use an invisible zipper foot, follow the manufacturer's instructions for installing the zipper.

8 Begin sewing at the pin that marks the start of the zipper teeth **(fig. 2)**. Drop the needle into the pillow and tape and remove the pin. Lower the presser foot and sew a few stitches, then backstitch to secure. Continue sewing along the length of the zipper, removing pins as you sew. Stop when the bottom of the zipper (the lower zipper stop) halts the presser foot. Backstitch to secure.

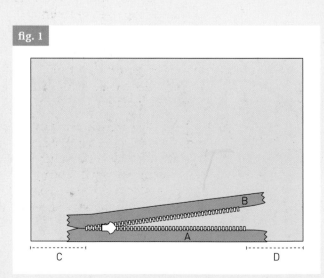

fig. 1

C   A   B   D

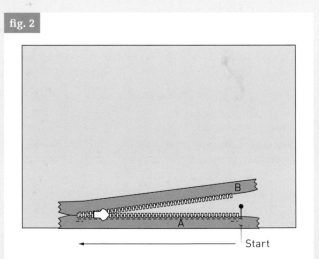

fig. 2

Start

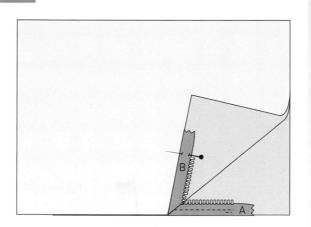

fig. 3

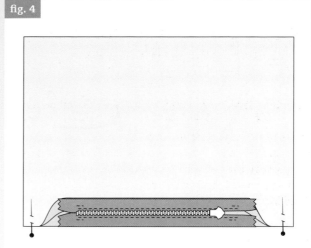

fig. 4

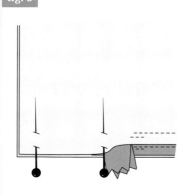

fig. 5

9   Layer the pillow back and front with right sides together. If the pillow back's fabric is directional, make sure the zipper is at the bottom.

10   Align Side B of the zipper tape **(fig. 1)** on the pillow back, right sides together, with edges matched and the teeth toward the center of the pillow.

11   Center the zipper on the bottom edge, using the measurement recorded earlier. To double check, measure again from the ends of the zipper to the edges of the backing when the zipper is pinned in place **(fig. 3)**.

12   Place a pin at the top of the zipper to mark where the zipper teeth begin. Adjust the needle to the other side of the zipper foot to sew Side B, again placing the stitches about ¹⁄₁₆" (1.5 mm) from the zipper teeth.

13   Repeat Step 7 to attach side B of the zipper to the pillow back.

14   Close the zipper and align the pillow corners; pin **(fig. 4)**.

15   Swivel and fold the loose ends of the zipper tape toward the pillow's raw edge and pin the top and backing together as close to the zipper stops as possible at both ends of the zipper **(fig. 5)**.

16   Unzip the zipper about two-thirds of its length. Pin the pillow top and back together around all four sides, keeping right sides together and aligning the raw edges.

17   Attach the walking foot to the sewing machine. Sew the pillow top and back together. Start with a ⅜" (1 cm) seam allowance, as close to the bottom of the zipper as possible. Sew a few stitches, backstitch to secure, and continue sewing until ½" (1.3 cm) from the corner.

18   Stop with the needle down, raise the presser foot, and turn the pillow 90 degrees. Continue sewing around the pillow with a ½" (1.3 cm) seam allowance, stopping ½" (1.3 cm) from the next two corners to turn. At the final corner, stop ⅜" (1 cm) from the edge of the pillow, turn the pillow 90 degrees, and continue sewing with a ⅜" (1 cm) seam allowance. End the stitching as close to the top of the zipper as possible and backstitch to secure.

19   Trim diagonally across the pillow corners to reduce bulk. Be sure not to cut into the stitches.

20   Open the zipper completely and turn the pillow right side out. Gently smooth the corners into position with a turning tool. Press. Insert the pillow form, zip the zipper, and enjoy!

free yourseLf
FREE-PIECING TECHNIQUE AND PROJECTS

Free piecing—a cycle of auditioning, cutting, sewing, and reviewing—is the foundation for improvisation and the process we used for all the quilts in this book. Some of the quilts are freer and more improvisational than others, but each evolved from an idea and went through several variations before we arrived at the finished quilt. This is an invigorating, trial-and-error process as you create a dialogue with your work.

Let instinct, intuition, and possibility be your guide. Release perfectionism and trust your ideas. Free yourself and let your fabrics work for you and speak to you. We audition fabrics on the design wall, placing them and then standing back to ponder, experiment, add and take away. Free piecing is a technique ripe for using scraps from other projects and for tapping into your creative side. Be fearless and push through any doubt.

free-piecing technique

Selecting and sewing two pieces of fabric together is the best way to get the intuitive feel of the free-piecing process. Experience will give you a better understanding of how color, value, and placement influence design. One decision will influence the next, and your quilt will take shape organically.

establish parameters

A blank design wall can be intimidating. Defining parameters before you begin a project can help you focus and tackle a project one step at a time. Parameters provide freedom within structure. Our tips for establishing parameters follow.

Use Magic Numbers. Perhaps you want to use different-sized blocks in your quilt, but you're not ready to move to anything-goes block sizes, or no blocks at all. Try this system of using block sizes that will fit together automatically for flexibility in design. For example, the combination of 3" (7.5 cm), 6" (15 cm), and 12" (30.5 cm) finished sizes is an example of what we call *magic numbers*. Blocks with sides in those three sizes, even rectangular blocks, will fit together without alteration and allow for many possible arrangements **(fig. 1)**. Use block sizes that fit together without alteration.

Choose a Block Size Visually. Tape a block's area on your design wall and work within the taped perimeter. Sometimes it's easier to visualize a design in a confined area.

Work Outside of the Block Structure. Quilts don't have to have blocks of the same size or even have blocks at all. Tape out the estimated finished size of the quilt you want to make and work within that area.

Paneling. Blocks of different sizes are fun to make, but putting them together may present a dilemma. What we call paneling is one solution. With paneling, blocks look randomly placed when sewn together, but have an underlying structure. The first step in paneling is to tape out a structure on the design wall and then place the blocks into the taped panels. The size of the panels can be adjusted to accommodate the blocks as long as the panels ultimately form squares and rectangles that can be sewn together easily. Begin by placing blocks along the panel edges, then move the blocks until you are satisfied. In **fig. 2**, we grouped seven blocks of varying sizes into panels, then assembled the panels to make the larger patchwork piece.

After you've placed the blocks, look to see where you need to add background fabric to create sections that can be sewn together. Assemble the blocks into squares and rectangles that fit together like a puzzle. The tape acts as a boundary for measuring and calculating background additions. Be aware of loss from seam allowances; multi-block layouts will shrink significantly as you sew them together. Construct the panel a bit larger than necessary and trim it to the finished size plus ¼" (6 mm) seam allowance all around. If your piece is too small, add to it; too large, trim to size.

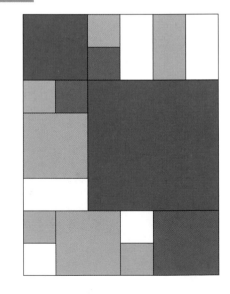

fig. 1

fig. 2

Add strips of fabric to equalize randomly sized blocks,
then assemble them into panels before completing the quilt top.

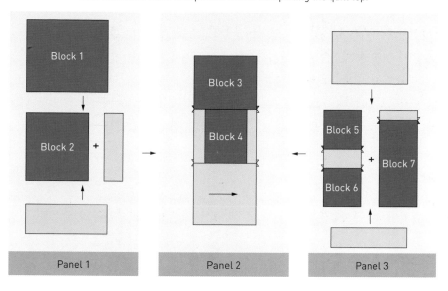

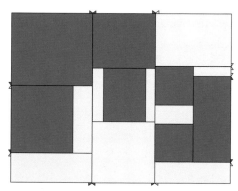

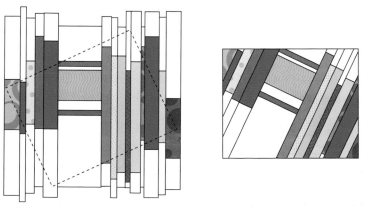

extend

You may need to enlarge blocks or pieces of fabric to fit into a design. *Extending* is simply adding fabric to increase the length or width of a block or section. In Panel 1 of **fig. 2**, fabric is added to the right side of block 2, extending it to the same width as block 1. The extension allows us to sew those blocks together.

trim

Trim to alter a design or fix a design that isn't working. Notice how the design in **fig. 3** changes by trimming it on an angle.

You could also cut apart the piece in **fig. 3** and sew the parts together in a different configuration. Have the courage to cut off parts of a design that may not be working. Be sure to place your trimmings back on the design wall, as they may find their way back into your piece in another spot.

fig. 3

Trim pieced units to alter or improve a design.

angle piecing

Creating angles will give you versatility in your piecing. We use three methods for angle piecing.

1   On your cutting mat, place piece A right side up. Place piece B right side down, at the desired angle across piece A. Align a ruler with the angle and trim the excess fabric from piece A with a rotary cutter **(fig. 4)**. Sew along the angle, using a ¼" (6 mm) seam allowance. Flip piece B right side up and press it away from piece A. This method is simple and works well when piecing fabrics randomly.

2   This method keeps the edges of the fabrics from skewing. Overlap two pieces of equal width, right sides up, overlapping enough to accommodate the desired angle. Cut the angle with a ruler and rotary cutter, cutting through both fabric layers **(fig. 5)**. Discard the small scraps from the ends of the pieces.

Place piece B on piece A, right sides together, aligning the newly cut edges **(fig. 6)**. Sew and press. The pieces join at an angle while the edges of the pieced unit remain straight.

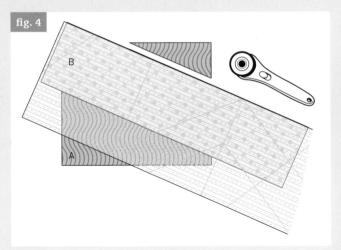

fig. 4

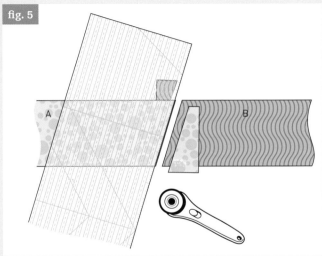

fig. 5

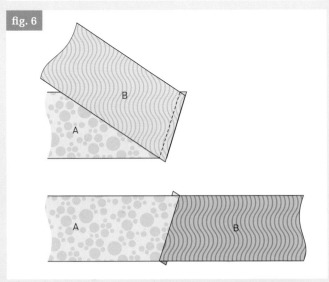

fig. 6

3 This method is a variation of the previous method. Instead of using two equal-width strips, one strip is a wider than the other. This eliminates the precise matching required in the previous method. Overlap the strips, right sides up, and trim the angle as before **(fig. 7)**. Place B on A with right sides together, aligning the angled edges **(fig. 8)**. Stitch, flip piece B into place, and press. Use a ruler to extend the edges of B across piece A and trim A to match, yielding straight edges.

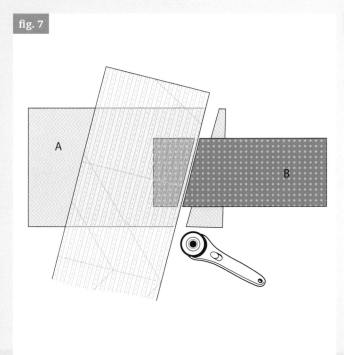

fig. 7

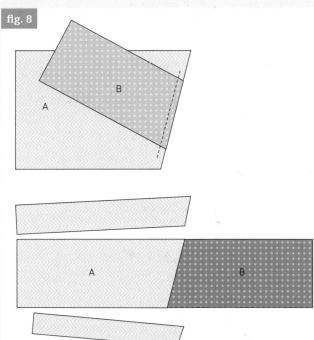

fig. 8

hints and tips

✢ Try to form squares and rectangles as you piece. These shapes are easier to fit together into larger units than irregular shapes.

✢ Your design wall is one of your most important tools and essential to free-piecing success. Step away from the project frequently to view it on the design wall from a distance—it's the best way to see value, color, and design.

urban garden quilt

finished size: 37" × 52" (94 × 132 cm)

We were inspired to make the Urban Garden quilt by a view of fields from the window of a plane. We took handfuls of orange, green, and brown scraps and started working on our design wall. As we placed and arranged the scraps, the fabric combinations began to appear to us as little plots in city gardens. We embraced the look and a quilt was born.

materials
All fabric amounts are for 45" (114.5 cm) wide fabric.

- 2½ yd (2.3 m) beige fabric for background
- ½ yd (45.5 cm) total of several orange, green, and brown fabrics
- 1⅔ yd (1.5 m) fabric for backing
- ⅓ yd (30.5 cm) fabric for binding
- 45" × 60" (114.5 × 152.5 cm) low-loft cotton batting

tools
- Modern quilter's toolbox (page 10)

cut the fabric

⚒ From binding fabric, cut 5 strips 2¼" (5.5 cm) × width of fabric.

construct the quilt

Note: Unless otherwise indicated, all seam allowances are ¼" (6 mm) and are pressed open.

The Urban Garden quilt is constructed in three columns containing a total of eleven panels, as shown in the construction diagram at right. Construct one panel at a time. Review the Free-Piecing technique on page 46.

1 Tape the perimeter of one panel on the design wall. The area within the tape should equal the finished size of the panel.

2 Gather the fabrics and sort by color. Place scraps or pieces cut from various fabrics on the design wall within the panel, arranging the pieces into small groupings and leaving plenty of open areas for the background fabric. Create contrast and interest with the arrangement of colors and values. The background fabric in each panel represents untilled areas of the garden. Consider the ratio of colorful fabrics to background fabric in each panel. As you build your design, keep in mind that you will lose ½" (1.3 cm) of each fabric in both dimensions to seam allowances, so the design will shrink significantly as you sew it together.

3 When you are satisfied with the arrangement, sew the patches together, adding background fabric as needed. As you join pieces, return them to the design wall and monitor the shrinkage caused by seam allowances, adding more pieces around the edges as needed. Construct the panel a bit larger than the taped area and trim back to the panel size, plus ¼" (6 mm) seam allowance all around.

4 If a section ends up too short, add to it. If a section is too long, trim it back. Trim each panel to size as it is constructed, adding ¼" (6 mm) seam allowance all around, and place it back into position within the quilt layout.

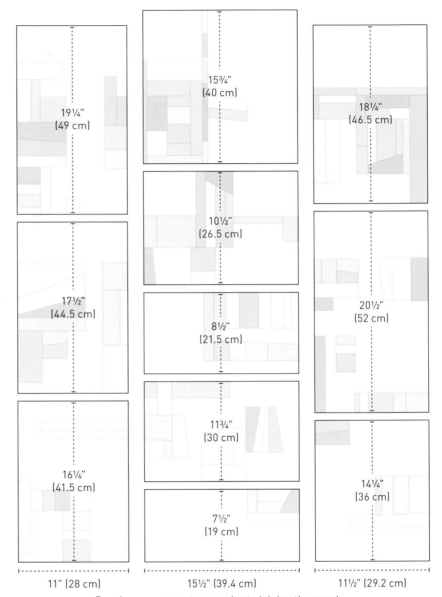

19¼" (49 cm)

15¾" (40 cm)

18¼" (46.5 cm)

17½" (44.5 cm)

10½" (26.5 cm)

8½" (21.5 cm)

20½" (52 cm)

16¼" (41.5 cm)

11¾" (30 cm)

7½" (19 cm)

14¼" (36 cm)

11" (28 cm)   15½" (39.4 cm)   11½" (29.2 cm)

Panel measurements are prior to joining the panels.

Urban Garden construction diagram

how to create a panel

These steps show how we created a panel for this quilt (your scrap sizes and placement will differ).

1 | Construct the center area first. Join pieces 1 and 2 along one long edge. Sew pieces 3 and 4 together, then add piece 5; join the unit to strips 1 and 2 **(fig. 1)**. Add piece 6 to the upper corner of the center section.

2 | Sew strips 7 and 8 together. Extend the top of this section with background fabric so it is the same height as the center section and sew the two sections together.

3 | Sew small pieces together to form the strip marked by the bracket in **fig. 1**. Extend the top of this section with background fabric to reach the height of the center section and sew it to the right side of the center section.

4 | Extend piece 11 by angle-piecing (page 50) a strip of background fabric to its right side. Add piece 12.

5 | Extend the 11+12 section with background fabric to equal the width of the top section.

6 | Sew background fabric to each side of piece 10 so that it measures the full height of the panel. Sew it to the right side of the assembled patches. The panel is complete **(fig. 2)**.

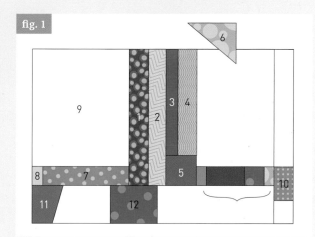

fig. 1

fig. 2

5 When all the panels are complete, sew the panels in each column together in order from top to bottom, with right sides together and raw edges matched.

6 Sew the three columns together in order from left to right to complete the quilt top.

7 Trim the selvedges from the backing fabric and press it to remove wrinkles.

8 On a flat surface, make a quilt sandwich by layering the backing fabric, batting, and the quilt top. Baste the layers together.

9 Quilt as desired. Trim the backing and batting to match the quilt top.

10 Join the binding strips to make a continuous length. Bind the raw edges to finish the quilt. See chapter 4 (page 32) for further instructions on basting and binding.

We used a walking foot to densely quilt the Urban Garden quilt with a serpentine stitch, a decorative stitch on our sewing machine that reminds us of plowed furrows.

sea glass quilt

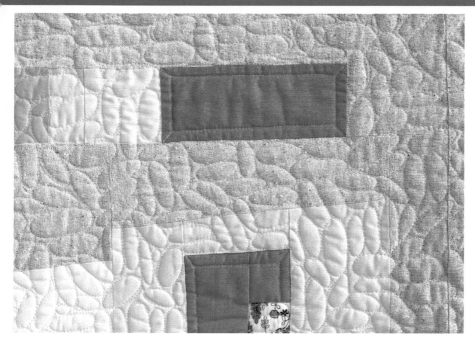

finished size: 54" × 60" (137 × 152.5 cm)

The cover of a book Jacquie purchased on a trip to Maine inspired the Sea Glass quilt. The colors of the beach and the soft blues, greens, and aquas set the mood and the color palette for the design. This quilt was made from scraps (as was the Urban Garden quilt on page 52), along with some leftover Log Cabin blocks (Log Cabin instructions begin on page 64). The background fabric is osnaburg, a cotton utility fabric with a wonderful texture.

materials
All fabric amounts are for 45" (114.5 cm) wide fabric.

- 3 yd (2.75 m) osnaburg for background
- ⅔ yd (61 cm) white fabric
- ½ yd (45.5 cm) aqua fabric
- ¼ yd (23 cm) turquoise fabric
- ¼ yd (23 cm) total of various blue/green print fabrics
- ½ yd (45.5 cm) total of various light green, medium green, dark green, and blue fabrics
- 3½ yd (3.2 m) fabric for backing
- ½ yd (45.5 cm) fabric for binding
- 62" × 68" (157.5 × 172.5 cm) low-loft cotton batting

tools
- Modern quilter's toolbox (page 10)

cut the fabric

Note: The fabrics for the quilt top were cut with scissors and no ruler, rather than with a rotary cutter, to give a slightly wavy feel to the edges of the piecing. Use a rotary cutter to cut the binding strips.

⁜ From binding fabric, cut 7 strips 2¼" (5.5 cm) × width of fabric.

⁜ From backing fabric, cut 2 lengths, each 62" (157.5 cm).

construct the quilt

Note: Unless otherwise indicated, all seam allowances are ¼" (6 mm) and are pressed open.

1   This quilt uses elongated wonky Log Cabin blocks that are cut apart in various ways and used as pieces in the quilt. Trim fabrics with scissors as needed. Make five elongated wonky Log Cabin blocks (see page 69) as shown in **fig. 1**, ranging from 9" × 15" (23 × 38 cm) to 12" × 18" (30.5 × 45.5 cm). Use a majority of solid fabrics with small pieces of the prints as accents. Our blocks have subtle wonkiness with white as the final round of logs to add brightness.

2   Tape the outlines of all the quilt panels on your design wall, following the construction diagram.

3   Cut the Log Cabin blocks apart vertically, horizontally, and at angles to create parts to use in the quilt. Cut each block once or multiple times. Divide one block at a time and place its parts in the taped outline on your design wall.

4   Continue cutting and placing until all the pieces have been placed in the quilt structure.

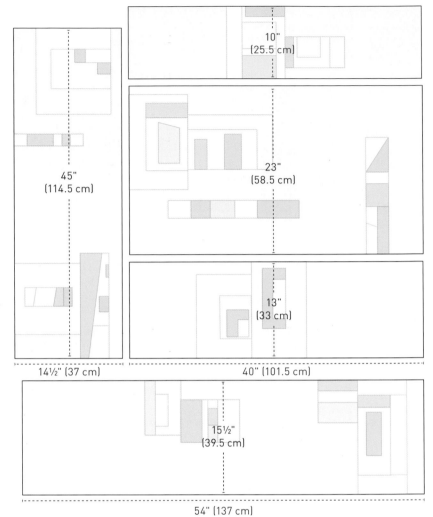

Panel measurements are prior to joining the panels.

Sea Glass construction diagram

Stand back and observe where additional sections need to be added.

5   Cut and join pieces of the solid and print fabrics to create additional sections in the quilt **(fig. 2)**. Use angle piecing, page 50, or gentle curved piecing, page 156, to add interest. Place each new section on the design wall as it is constructed. Add, cut, and rearrange sections until you are satisfied with the composition.

6   Measure the pieced sections and cut background fabric as needed to construct the panels. Make each panel a bit larger than its taped area and trim to size as each panel is completed (seam allowances are included in the measurements shown above).

7   When all the panels are complete, construct the upper right column of the structure by sewing its panels together from top to bottom. Pin, aligning raw edges. Sew and press.

fig. 1

fig. 2

panel construction

To create the panel in **fig. 3**:

1 | A, the grayed area, is part of a Log Cabin block. The right side of A has been cut off at an angle.

2 | Construct the pieced section to the right of A as a rectangle; later it will be angle pieced to A.

3 | Sew piece 1 to a white scrap (piece 2). Sew this unit to the bottom of piece 3 and trim the edges to match.

4 | Sew piece 4 to the right side of the assembled unit so that it extends a few inches beyond the taped edge of the panel. The extra fabric will accommodate the angle piecing.

5 | Sew pieces 5 and 6 to the top and bottom of the pieced unit and trim the raw edges to match.

6 | Extend the top and bottom of the pieced section with background fabric (pieces 7 and 8) so it continues a few inches beyond the taped panel edges.

7 | Angle piece this entire section to the right side of A.

8 | Cut and sew a background strip (piece 9) the height of the panel, to the left side of A. Trim the panel to size, including ¼" (6 mm) seam allowances on the outer edges.

8 Place the left panel on the assembled column, right sides together. Pin, aligning the raw edges. Sew and press. Sew the bottom panel to the assembled unit and press to complete the quilt top.

9 Trim the selvedges from the backing fabric. Sew the two 62" (157.5 cm) lengths together along one long edge, using a ½" (1.3 cm) seam allowance. Press. Trim to 62" × 68" (157.5 × 173 cm), centering the seam.

10 Make a quilt sandwich from the backing, batting, and quilt top. Baste the layers together.

11 Quilt as desired. Trim the backing and batting to match the quilt top.

12 Join the binding strips to make a continuous length. Bind the raw edges to finish the quilt. See chapter 4 (page 32) for further instructions on basting and binding.

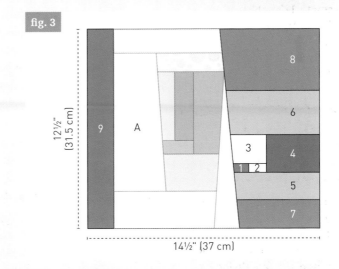

fig. 3

12½" (31.5 cm)

14½" (37 cm)

Elongated quilted pebbles fill the background of the Sea Glass quilt, creating texture reminiscent of a sandy beach.

winging it pillow

finished size: 18" × 18" (45.5 × 45.5 cm); variation pillows shown are 22" × 14" (56 × 35.5 cm) and 19" × 19" (48.5 × 48.5 cm).

Do you love digging through and admiring your beloved scraps? Free piecing gives all those lovely scraps a home! A single piece of Katie's butterfly fabric inspired the Winging It pillow. We then found fabrics in our scrap bins to showcase the butterfly. The design of the pillow emerged as we placed fabrics on the design wall and worked through the free-piecing process. The final design resembles a butterfly's spreading wings. This small project will give you insight into free piecing.

materials

All fabric amounts are for 45" (114.5 cm) wide fabric.
Amounts listed will make one pillow.

- Focus-fabric scrap (shown: 4¼" × 4½" [11 × 11.5 cm] approximate finished size)
- ⅓ yd (30.5 cm) total of various print and solid-color fabrics that coordinate with the focus fabric
- ½ yd (45.5 cm) background fabric (shown: natural osnaburg)
- ⅔ yd (61 cm) fabric for pillow backing
- 24" × 24"(61 × 61 cm) low-loft cotton batting
- ⅔ yd (61 cm) muslin
- 18" × 18" (45.5 × 45.5 cm) pillow form
- 16" (40.5 cm) invisible zipper (shorten as needed)

tools

- Modern quilter's toolbox (page 10)
- Zipper foot (or optional invisible zipper foot) for sewing machine

cut the fabric

※ From backing fabric, cut 1 square 19" × 19" (48.5 × 48.5 cm).

※ From muslin, cut 1 square 22" × 22" (56 × 56 cm).

※ Cut the focus-fabric scrap into a four-sided shape large enough to be the focal point of the pillow.

※ Cut about 15 various print and solid fabrics into wedges or consistent-width strips, with widths ranging from ¾" to 4" (2 to 10 cm) and lengths up to 16" (40.5 cm). Our scraps were mostly medium values so we added some solids to create contrast and definition. More scraps can be added as needed, and fabrics may be repeated.

construct the pillow top

Note: Unless otherwise indicated, all seam allowances are ¼" (6 mm) and are pressed open.

1 Tape a 20" (51 cm) square on the design wall to help you place the fabrics as you create a design within the dimensions of the pillow top.

2 To focus maximum attention on the butterfly, we framed it with contrasting print and background fabrics above and below the butterfly print, as detailed in Steps 3 through 5.l/

3 Cut two strips each of print and background fabrics, any width, with their lengths roughly equal to the width of the focus fabric.

4 Place the background-fabric strips on the top and bottom of the focus-fabric piece, right sides together. Sew and press the seams.

5 Sew the print strips to the top and bottom of the pieced unit at an angle, using either of the angle-piecing techniques explained on page 50.

6 Place the focus-fabric unit where you would like it to appear on the pillow, within the taped area on the design wall. Working from the focus fabric toward both sides, surround the butterfly unit with solid fabrics and prints that create contrast **(fig. 1)**.

7 Measure from each strip to the tapes at top and bottom, as shown in **fig. 2**, to determine approximate lengths for the background strips necessary to extend the print/solid strips. Add ½" (1.3 cm) to the measurement for seam allowances, but don't worry about being exact. Cut each background strip a bit wider

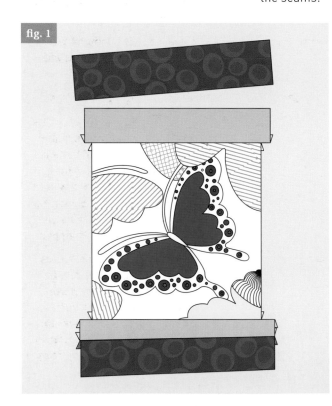

fig. 1

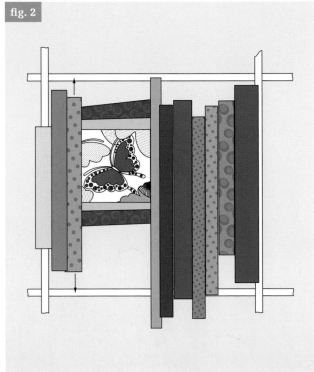

fig. 2

than the contrasting fabric strip to which it will be sewn.

8 Sew a background strip to each end of the corresponding print or solid strip, right sides together, and press **(fig. 3)**. Trim each assembled strip so its long side edges are straight.

9 Place the extended strips back on the design wall. Starting at the right edge of the focus fabric unit, join the strips in succession along their straight edges, or angle piece them. We angled some of the strips to create movement and a free feeling.

10 Continue sewing strips together to fill the taped area. We added an additional background fabric strip to one side of the pieced unit to reach the desired size.

11 Trim the pieced fabric to 19" (48.5 cm) square to finish the pillow top.

12 Make a quilt sandwich with the muslin square, batting, and the pieced fabric.

13 Baste and quilt as desired.

14 After the pillow top is quilted, trim the muslin and batting to match the pieced pillow top. Complete the pillow with backing fabric and zipper. See page 44 for instructions on inserting an invisible zipper.

We chose minimal quilting for this pillow. In general, pillows require less quilting than quilts because their layers won't shift as much in use. The quilting boldly echoes the outside shape of the free piecing in a decorative triple stitch in contrasting thread. ✢

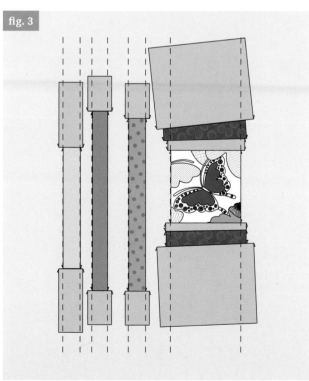

fig. 3

Log cabin makeover

IMPROVISATIONAL LOG CABIN TECHNIQUE AND PROJECTS

The popular traditional Log Cabin block lends itself to modern interpretation. The classic block has a square center surrounded by sets of fabric strips—called rounds of logs—that are the same width throughout the block. The wonderful secondary designs in Log Cabin quilts come from value differences on each side of the blocks; traditional Log Cabin blocks are pieced with light values on one side and dark values on the opposite side. Quilting lore says that a red center represents the hearth of the cabin, while the light is the sunny side of the cabin, and the dark is the cabin in shadow.

◀ Mod TV quilt, page 70

log cabin technique

Traditional Log Cabin blocks are pieced in one of three patterns: spiraling outward from the center, courthouse steps style, or in the pineapple version, as shown below. Each of these Log Cabin varieties is ripe for a modern makeover.

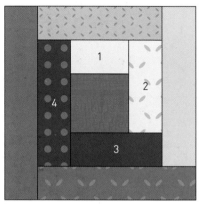

The traditional **Spiraling** Log Cabin block adds logs around the center in succession, to complete one round of logs.

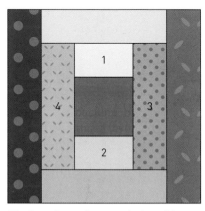

The **Courthouse Steps** variation adds logs to the top and bottom and then to the sides to complete one round of logs.

The **Pineapple** Log Cabin block variation adds logs to the corners as well as the top, bottom, and sides.

Instructions for modern Log Cabin variations follow; these are the types of blocks you'll use in the projects in this chapter as well as in a few other quilts in this book. To practice these variations, gather large scraps or fat quarters of several fabrics, a rotary cutter, cutting mat, a 24" (61 cm) acrylic quilter's ruler, and a 12½" (31.5 cm) square acrylic quilter's ruler.

basic wonky log cabin block

Log Cabin blocks in the improvisational quilting style disregard traditional light and dark value placements and use consistent-width and skewed logs, strips in a variety of widths, and inserts. The following steps show basic skewing of a classic Log Cabin block to create a modern Wonky Log Cabin block **(fig. 1)**. This block uses the spiraling method.

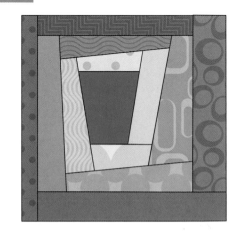

fig. 1

1   Begin with a finished block size in mind. Knowing the finished block size in advance will help you calculate the strip widths for the final round of logs. Our sample block finishes 12" (30.5 cm) square.

2   Cut a four-sided shape as the center strip. Cut a strip a bit longer than the center's width

and at least 1" (2.5 cm) wide **(fig. 2)**. Wider strips allow more flexibility for cutting angles in the strips. This is log 1 in the image.

3 Sew the strip to the top of the center fabric strip, right sides together, using a ¼" (6 mm) seam allowance. Press the seam open.

4 Align a ruler with the right edge of the center strip and trim to create a straight edge through both pieces **(fig. 3)**.

5 Cut a strip for log 2 a bit longer than the right side of your sewn unit. Sew the strip to the right edge of the sewn unit,

right sides together. Press and trim even with the top and bottom edges **(fig. 4)**.

6 Repeat the process of cutting, sewing, pressing, and trimming to add log 3 to the bottom and log 4 to the left side, completing one round of logs. Notice how different width logs add interest to the block **(fig. 5)**.

7 Skew the block and create some wonkiness. Use the strip for the next log to audition the angle before you cut the top of the block by simply laying it on the pieced unit, right sides up **(fig. 6)**. Angles may be slight

or acute. Remove the strip and make the cut across the pieced unit, remembering to add seam allowances.

8 Reposition the new strip on the pieced unit, right sides together, matching the raw edges. Stitch and press, and the wonkiness is revealed. Continue adding strips around the spiral, skewing the strips as desired to complete the next round of logs.

9 Add the third round of logs, repeating the spiral: top, right, bottom and then the left side. In the illustration, this round of logs is not skewed **(fig. 7)**.

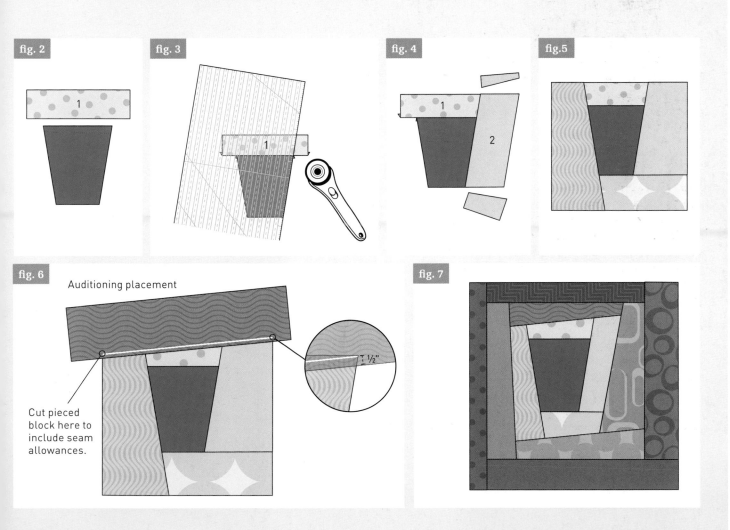

fig. 2

fig. 3

1

fig. 4

1 2

fig.5

fig. 6

Auditioning placement

Cut pieced block here to include seam allowances.

1½"

fig. 7

fig. 8

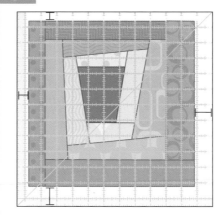

fig. 9

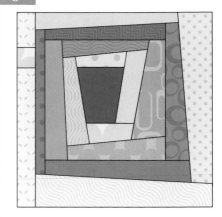

10 Place a 12½" (31.5 cm) square ruler over the block to estimate the width of the strips for the final round of logs. Notice that the block doesn't have to be centered under the ruler **(fig. 8)**. When calculating strip widths, add ½" (1.3 cm) to the width of each log for seam allowances. If you plan to skew the strips, cut them wider to take the angle into account. We like to cut strips larger than necessary; it's easy to trim back.

fig. 10

11 After adding the final round of logs, again in the spiraling pattern (top, right, bottom, left) use the square ruler to trim the block to 12½" (31.5 cm) square **(fig. 9)**.

12 In the block in **fig. 9,** notice that we added an insert to one of the logs in the final round. The insert adds a bit of surprise to an ordinary block and is a fun way to showcase a print. To create an insert, cut a strip. Slice it where you want the insert to appear. Sew one half of the strip to each side of the insert **(fig. 10)**. Trim the insert to match the strip edges and use the sewn unit as a log in your Wonky Log Cabin block.

hints and tips

✤ Think about the width of the logs when trimming at an angle. Part of a log will disappear into the seam allowance if it is trimmed to less than ½" (1.3 cm) wide.

✤ Contrast between rounds of logs allows the design to shine. Audition logs before you cut to see how the values work together.

✤ Choose a focus fabric for the center. The Log Cabin block is a good way to showcase novelty or large-scale print fabrics.

✤ When adding strips to severely angled logs, be sure to cut extra strip width to accommodate the angle.

✤ When cutting a severe angle across a log, replace the fabric you remove in the cut with another log (or multiple logs) on that side, or increase the width of the next log.

✤ If you don't own the correct size ruler, tape an area on your design wall the desired size of the block. Place your partially completed block within the taped area to calculate the final strip widths.

variations

It's easy to alter the Log Cabin block. With imagination and some trial and error we're sure that you'll be inventing your own unique version. Here are some of the variations we use in our quilts.

elongated wonky log cabin

Elongate any Log Cabin block style into a rectangle rather than the traditional square. Use wider strips for the top and bottom logs and narrower strips for the side logs or start with an elongated center. We used elongated blocks in the Tunnel Vision quilt on page 78 and the Sea Glass quilt on page 56.

minimalist log cabin

Minimalist Log Cabin blocks are constructed courthouse-style. Using only one round of logs and replacing one log in the center or outer round with a print or a contrasting solid gives this block a clean, minimalist feel. Subtle skewing is characteristic of these blocks. We used Minimalist Log Cabin blocks in the Lilac Crush quilt on page 74.

tunnel log cabin

The Tunnel Log Cabin block uses the spiraling method and creates the feel of a tunnel with narrow, consistent-width strips on adjacent sides of the block. The logs on the opposite side are various widths and can be wonky or straight. Tunnel blocks look best in solid fabrics and can create interesting illusions in a quilt. See the Tunnel Vision quilt on page 78.

weighted log cabin

Use wider strips on one side of the block to create the Weighted Log Cabin block. These blocks work better in a horizontal elongated format. The Mod TV quilt on page 70 uses this variation.

Elongated Wonky Log Cabin Block

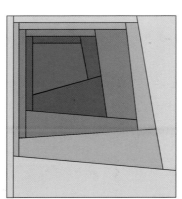

Two versions of the Tunnel Log Cabin Block

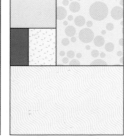
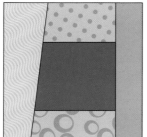

Two versions of the Minimalist Log Cabin Block

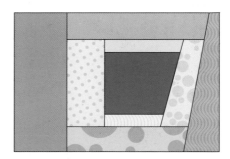

Weighted Log Cabin Block

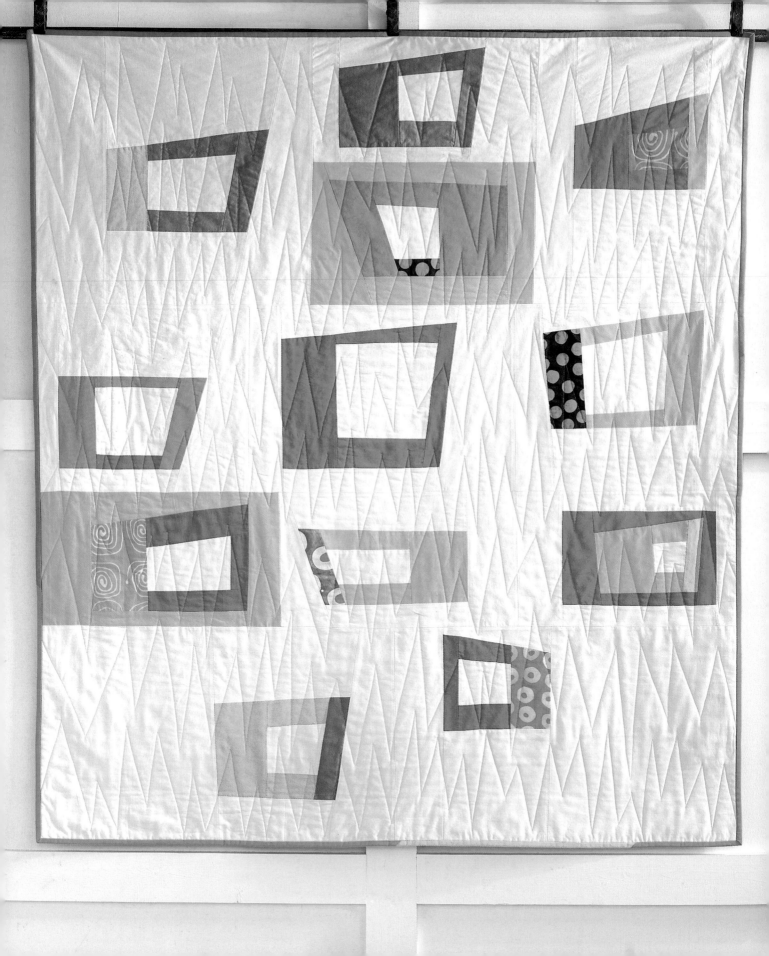

mod tv quilt

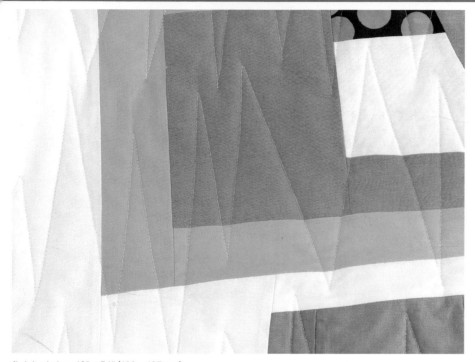

finished size: 48" × 54" (122 × 137 cm)

A vintage Philco television, with its side-mounted speaker and signature screen shape, inspired the Mod TV quilt. The Weighted Log Cabin block variation has a shape similar to the Philco and a mid-century modern feel that we thought was perfect for this quilt. The bright, welcoming color scheme makes for a very appealing quilt.

materials
All fabric amounts are for 45" (114.5 cm) wide fabric.

- 2½ yd (2.3 m) white fabric
- ¼ yd (23 cm) dark turquoise fabric
- ¼ yd (23 cm) medium turquoise fabric
- ½ yd (45.5 cm) light turquoise fabric
- ⅛ yd (11.5 cm) total of various turquoise print fabric scraps
- ⅛ yd (11.5 cm) grass green fabric
- ⅛ yd (11.5 cm) lime green fabric
- 2¾ yd (2.5 m) fabric for backing
- ½ yd (45.5 cm) fabric for binding
- 56" × 62" (142 × 157.5 cm) low-loft cotton batting

tools
- Modern quilter's toolbox (page 10)

cut the fabric

* From binding fabric, cut 5 strips 2¼" (5.5 cm) × width of fabric.

* From backing fabric, cut 1 length 63" (160 cm) × width of fabric. From remaining fabric, cut 2 lengths 17" × width of fabric.

construct the quilt

Note: Unless otherwise indicated, all seam allowances are ¼" (6 mm) and are pressed open.

1 Mod TV contains twelve Weighted Log Cabin blocks (see page 69) set randomly within a paneled structure. The majority of the blocks have a center, one round of colored logs, and a final round of white logs. A couple of the blocks have two rounds of colored logs.

2 Have the white, solid color, and print fabrics near your cutting mat. Cut twelve centers for the blocks; eleven of our centers are white and one is cut from a print fabric. Centers can be squares, rectangles, or asymmetric shapes as shown in **fig. 1**; this shape establishes one angled side of the TV screen. Centers can be any size you choose—a variety of sizes make a more interesting quilt design.

3 Cutting strips as needed, sew one round of colored logs to

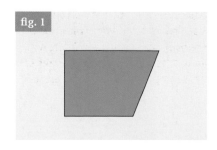

fig. 1

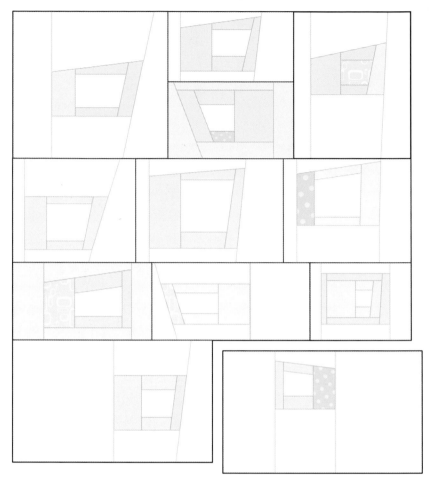

Improvise the size of the blocks for this quilt as described in the instructions.

Mod TV construction diagram

each center. Use turquoise for the majority of the blocks, with a couple of green blocks to add a little sparkle to the quilt. We also added a few print logs to some of the blocks for added interest.

4 Our blocks are placed randomly within panels, as shown in the construction diagram above. With paneling, the blocks appear randomly placed when sewn together, but the quilt actually has an underlying structure.

5 Because of the improvisational nature of the blocks, your block sizes will differ from ours; improvise the setting of your blocks accordingly. Follow the construction diagram or use it as a guide to create a structure of your own. Tape out the structure on your design wall. Adjust the size of the horizontal panels and the sections within panels to accommodate your block sizes.

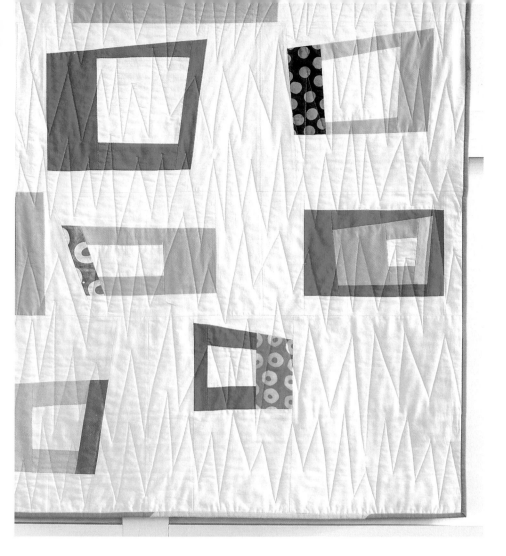

moving on to the next block. Remember to leave ¼" (6 mm) seam allowance on all sides when trimming the block.

11 When the panels are complete, sew them together in sections to make four horizontal panels. Join the panels from top to bottom to complete the quilt top. Pin each seam, right sides together, aligning the edges; sew and press.

12 Trim the selvedges from the backing fabric. Sew the two pieces 17" (43 cm) pieces together along the 17" (43 cm) sides using a ½" (1.3 cm) seam allowance. Press. Trim the unit to measure 63" (160 cm) long. (If your quilt is a different size, adjust backing accordingly.)

13 Sew the two backing units, right sides together, along one long edge, using a ½" (1.3 cm) seam allowance, and press.

14 Make a quilt sandwich from the backing, batting, and quilt top. Baste.

15 Quilt as desired. Trim the backing and batting to match the quilt top.

16 Join the binding strips to make a continuous length. Bind the raw edges to finish the quilt. See chapter 4 (page 32) for further instructions on basting and binding.

Inspired by the static that used to occur on old televisions when there was no programming available, we quilted the Mod TV quilt with rows of random zigzags across the quilt. ✚

6 Place the twelve blocks within the taped panels, moving them within the panels until you are satisfied with their placement.

7 Remove one block from the quilt structure at a time and sew a second round of logs to each block to fill the remaining space in its panel. Most of the blocks use white for the second round of logs, while a couple employ a different shade of turquoise.

8 As an example of making one panel, follow Steps 8, 9, and 10. Measure from the top and bottom edges of the block to the tape to calculate the strip widths, and cut strips a bit longer than the current block width. Sew the strips to the top and bottom of the pieced unit and press.

9 Measure from the sides of the block to the tape to calculate strip widths and cut strips long enough to span from upper tape to lower. Sew the strips to the sides.

10 We like the simplicity of only a few rounds of logs. Your blocks can have as few as ours or as many as you like. Trim each block to the desired height and width and replace it in the taped quilt structure before

Lilac crush quilt

finished size: 40" × 48½" (101.5 × 123 cm)

The modern, subtly off-kilter feel of the Minimalist Log Cabin block variation (page 69) inspired this simple but sophisticated baby quilt. Touches of lilac and violet add a feminine touch, and the gentle curves of the free-pieced pod border soften the hard edges of the Log Cabin blocks to create a soft, inviting feel.

materials

All fabric amounts are for 45" (114.5 cm) wide fabric.

- 2⅔ yd (2.5 m) cream fabric for background
- ⅔ yd (61 cm) brown fabric
- ½ yd (45.5 cm) beige fabric
- ¼ yd (23 cm) lilac print fabric
- ¼ yd (23 cm) total of several lilac and violet print fabrics
- 2¼ yd (2.1 m) fabric for backing
- ⅓ yd (30.5 cm) fabric for binding
- 48" × 56½" (122 × 143.5 cm) low-loft cotton batting

tools

- Modern quilter's toolbox (page 10)
- 12½" (31.5 cm) square ruler

cut the fabric

✳ From lilac print, cut 2 strips 2½"
(6.5 cm) × width of fabric.

✳ From background fabric, cut
3 strips 3½" (9 cm) × width of
fabric.

✳ From brown fabric, cut 4
centers.

✳ From beige fabric, cut 5 centers.

✳ From print scraps, cut 2 centers.

✳ From backing fabric, cut:

  ▸ 2 pieces 25" × 40"
  (63.5 × 101.5 cm)

  ▸ 2 pieces 17" × 25"
  (43 × 63.5 cm).

✳ From binding fabric, cut 5 strips
2¼" (5.5 cm) × width of fabric.

construct the quilt

*Note: Unless otherwise indicated, all
seam allowances are ¼" (6 mm) and
are pressed open.*

1 Lilac Crush consists of twelve
Minimalist Log Cabin blocks,
characterized by a center, two
rounds of logs, and straight
seams or subtle wonkiness. In
most blocks we used a print
fabric as one log in the first
round of logs and the cream
background fabric for the
second round of logs **(fig. 1)** so
the blocks appear to float on
the background.

2 Have your remaining
background, brown, and beige
fabrics and other scraps at
the cutting mat. Cut strips for
blocks as needed.

3 Follow the instructions in
Steps 4 and 5 to make seven
blocks with a print fabric as
one of the logs in the first
round and five blocks using the

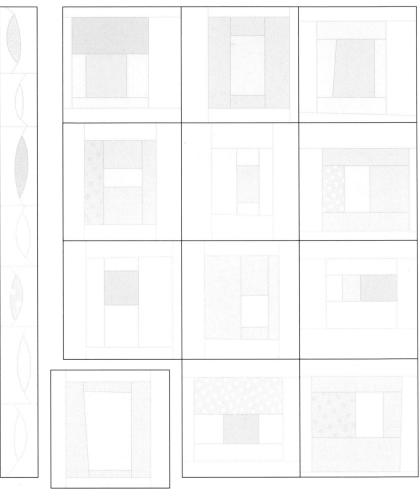

Each block measures 12½" (31.5 cm) square before blocks are joined.

Lilac Crush construction diagram

same solid fabric for all four
of the logs in the first round.
As shown, half of the blocks
have a majority of brown in the
first round of logs, and half
have a majority of beige. You'll
alternate the placement of the
blocks in the quilt by the color
of the first round of logs as
shown in the photograph on
page 74.

4 Sew the first round of logs
to the center, courthouse-
steps-style **(fig. 2)**. Trim
subtle angles into the strips
if desired.

5 When the first round is
complete, place the 12½"
(31.5 cm) ruler on the block
and estimate the strip
widths for the final round of
cream logs, including seam
allowances **(fig. 3)**. The block
doesn't have to be centered
within the ruler; strips of
different widths within the
round of logs create an
interesting look.

6 Trim the blocks to 12½"
(31.5 cm) square. Place
them on the design wall as
shown in the construction
diagram above.

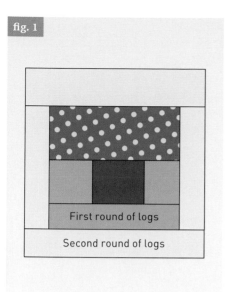

fig. 1

First round of logs

Second round of logs

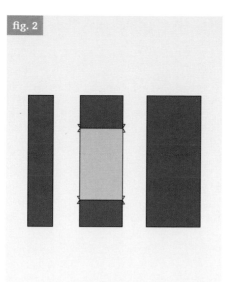

fig. 2

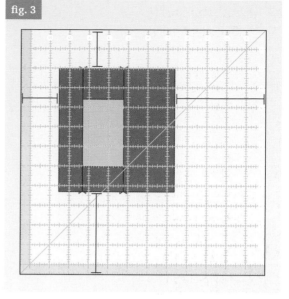

fig. 3

7 Sew the blocks into rows, aligning raw edges and keeping the placements as planned. Press. Place each completed row back on the design wall in the correct position.

8 Sew the rows together in order from top to bottom, aligning raw edges and matching seams. Press.

9 Use the lilac strips and cream background strips to make improvised pod blocks (page 157) for the border, as detailed in Steps 10, 11, and 12.

10 Cut seven rectangles from the lilac print in various sizes from about 4" to 7" (10 to 18 cm) long. Cut the pod shapes from the rectangles.

11 Cut two cream background rectangles for each pod shape, at least 3" (7.5 cm) longer than the pod. Make the pod blocks.

12 Trim each block into a rectangle 4" (10 cm) wide and as long as possible.

13 Place the pod blocks vertically along the left edge of the quilt top in a pleasing arrangement. Sew the blocks together along their short sides to create the border. Press and trim to 48½" (123 cm) long. If necessary, extend the pod border with background fabric to achieve the correct length.

14 Sew the border to the left side of the quilt, right sides together, aligning raw edges and matching corners. Press to finish the quilt top.

15 Sew the two 25" × 40" (63.5 × 101.5 cm) backing rectangles together along one long side, right sides together, using a ½" (1.3 cm) seam allowance. Press.

16 Sew the two 17" × 25" (43 × 63.5 cm) backing pieces, right sides together, along one short edge, using a ½" (1.3 cm) seam allowance. Press. Sew this strip to the bottom of the larger backing unit to complete the back of the quilt.

17 Make a quilt sandwich with the backing, batting, and quilt top. Baste the layers together.

18 Quilt as desired. Trim the backing and batting to match the quilt top.

19 Join the binding strips to make a continuous length. Bind the raw edges to finish the quilt. See chapter 4 (page 32) for further instructions on basting and binding.

Angela quilted the Lilac Crush quilt on a long-arm quilting machine with a delicate floral motif across the entire quilt. ✦

tunnel vision quilt

finished size: 64" × 83" (164 × 210 cm)

The Tunnel Log Cabin block variation, described on page 69, inspired the medallion-based design of this minimalist quilt. We featured the illusion of depth and movement that occurs when placing these types of blocks together. Four oversized blocks create a striking focal point. Each block begins with a dark center and logs lighten as they proceed outward. The subtle variations in value create a quiet yet dramatic statement.

materials
All fabric amounts are for 45" (114.5 cm) wide fabric.

- 1 fat eighth (9" × 22" [23 × 56 cm]) or ¼ yd (23 cm) of dark brown fabric
- 6 neutral fabrics in graduated values from light (#1) to dark (#6):
  - ⅔ yd (61 cm) fabric #1
  - ½ yd (45.5 cm) fabric #2
  - ⅓ yd (30.5 cm) fabric #3
  - ⅓ yd (30.5 cm) fabric #4
  - ¼ yd (23 cm) fabric #5
  - ¼ yd (23 cm) fabric #6
- 4 yd (3.7 m) fabric for background
- 4¾ yd (4.4 m) fabric for backing
- ⅝ yd (57 cm) fabric for binding
- 72" × 91" (183 × 231 cm) low-loft cotton batting

tools
- Modern quilter's toolbox (page 10)

cut the fabric

✳ From background fabric, cut:

➤ 1 strip 17½" (44.5 cm) × width of fabric, then cross-cut this strip as follows:

+ 2 strips 4½" × 17½" (11.5 × 44.5 cm) for A

+ 2 strips 9½" × 17½" (24 × 44.5 cm) for B

➤ 2 strips 15½" × 39½" (39.5 × 100.5 cm) for C

➤ 4 strips 22" × 32½" (56 × 82.5 cm) for D.

✳ From binding fabric, cut 8 strips 2¼" (5.5 cm) × width of fabric.

✳ From backing fabric, cut 2 strips 12" (30.5 cm) × width of fabric, then cut remaining backing fabric into two 72" (183 cm) lengths.

construct the quilt

Note: All seam allowances are ¼" (6 mm). Press seams open unless otherwise indicated.

1 The Tunnel Vision quilt is made from four skewed Tunnel Log Cabin blocks (page 69), each with a finished size of 13" × 17" (33 × 43 cm). Each block has a center strip and six rounds of logs. The logs on two adjacent sides are ½" (1.3 cm) wide and the opposite sides have skewed strips of various widths. The centers of each block are elongated four-sided shapes, resulting in elongated blocks. The centers are dark brown and the strips lighten in value with each round of logs. The logs are added in the spiraling pattern: top, right, bottom, and left.

2 Tape a 13½" × 17½" (34.5 × 44.5 cm) rectangle on your

Each of the four pieced center blocks measures 13½" × 17½" (34.5 × 44.5 cm) before blocks are joined.

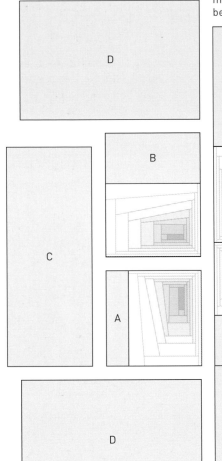
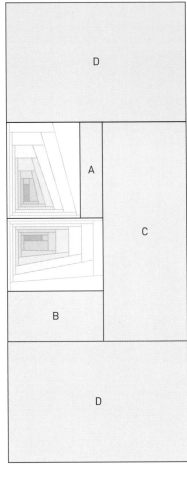

Tunnel Vision construction diagram

design wall and have the brown and neutral fabrics at the cutting mat. Cut four rectangular centers for the blocks from brown fabric, each about 1½" × 3½" (3.8 × 9 cm). Cut a 1" (2.5 cm) × width of fabric strip from each of the neutral fabrics for the fixed-width logs; cut additional strips as needed during piecing. Cut strips as needed for the variable-width logs, ranging in width from 1½" to 4" (3.8 to 10 cm).

3 Using the dimensions specified in Step 2, make four tunnel-style Log Cabin blocks. Skew the strips as desired. As you complete each round of logs, place the block in the taped area as shown in **fig. 1** to monitor the size of the block and to help estimate strip widths for the remaining rounds of logs.

4 Trim each block to 13½" × 17½" (34.5 × 44.5 cm). Trim only from the sides of the

block with variable-width logs. Place the four blocks on the design wall as shown in the construction diagram on page 80.

5 Sew two D background pieces along one short end to make a panel 22" × 64½" (56 × 164 cm). Repeat with the remaining D

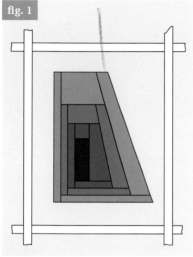

fig. 1

sections. Place background sections A, B, C, and D on the design wall according to the construction diagram.

6 Sew the A and B panels to the sides of the corresponding tunnel blocks and press. Replace these sections on the design wall in the correct positions.

7 Flip unit 1 onto unit 2, as shown in **fig. 2**, right sides together, aligning the raw edges. Sew the sections together and press. Repeat for the other two block units. Place them in position on the design wall.

8 Complete the center medallion by joining the assembled units, right sides together, along the center seam. Press.

9 Sew a C background piece to each side of the center

medallion, right sides together, aligning edges and corners. Press.

10 Sew the assembled D sections to the top and bottom of the medallion, right sides together, aligning edges and corners. Press to complete the quilt top.

11 Remove the selvedges from the backing fabric. Sew the two 12" (30.5 cm) strips together with a ½" (1.3 cm) seam along one short edge, press, and trim the strip to 72" (183 cm) long to make the first backing panel.

12 Sew the two 72" (183 cm) lengths of backing fabric together along one long edge using a ½" (1.3 cm) seam. Press. Sew the Step 11 panel to one long edge of this panel with a ½" (1.3 cm) seam and press to complete the quilt back.

13 Make a quilt sandwich with the backing, batting, and quilt top. Baste the layers.

14 Quilt as desired. Trim the backing and batting to match the quilt top.

15 Join the binding strips to make a continuous length. Bind the raw edges to finish the quilt. See chapter 4 (page 32) for further instructions on basting and binding.

We quilted the Tunnel Vision quilt with straight diagonal lines forming a double crosshatch. This adds beautiful texture, but allows the tunnel blocks to remain the focus of the quilt. ✛

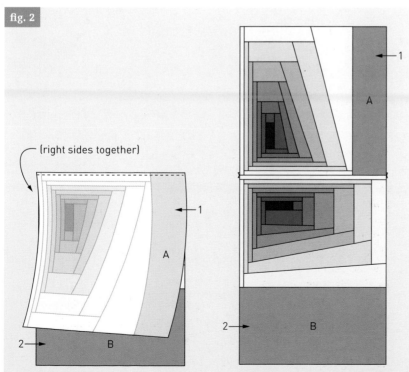

fig. 2

(right sides together)

1

A

2 → B

1

A

2 → B

slice and dice

SLICE AND INSERT
TECHNIQUE AND PROJECTS

The Slice and Insert technique is easy to master
and has unlimited design potential. With it you can
create both simple and intricate designs simply by
starting with pieces of fabric and progressively
slicing and inserting strips until the design appears.
More possibilities arise by combining different
strip widths and strip shapes. In this chapter we'll
demonstrate the skills needed for the Slice and Insert
technique and share a few of the tips we've learned.
Master these and you can make the quilts and pillows
in this section as well as your own designs. Have fun
slicing, dicing, and recombining!

slice and insert technique

To practice this technique and its variations, assemble scraps of fabric, your rotary cutter, cutting mat, and acrylic quilter's rulers, and your sewing machine.

basic slice and insert

Start with a piece of fabric slightly larger than the desired finished block size. Blocks are trimmed to size after insertions. You can work with any shape as the background, but we like working with squares or rectangles. The insert strips can be any width. Consistent-width strips are easiest, but you can use wedge-shaped strips; be sure to read the special instructions for using wedges as inserts on page 87.

1 Use a rotary cutter to slice the background fabric where you want the insert to appear. Measure the cut from edge to edge and cut the insert strip a little bit longer. Place the insert strip on the cut edge of A **(fig. 1)**, right sides together and raw edges matched, and sew.

2 Press the seam open unless the strip is less than 1" (2.5 cm) wide after insertion; in that case, press the seam allowances away from the strip.

3 Place section B on the inset, right sides together and raw edges matched **(fig. 2)**. Sew and press the seam.

4 Tada! You've inserted your first strip **(fig. 3)**. Trim the strip ends even with the background edges to complete.

matching seams

In many designs, insert strips will eventually intersect each other. To achieve the look of continuous lines, match the seams carefully.

1 Slice the block to create two sections, marked C and D in **fig. 4**. Sew the insert strip to the cut edge of C and press.

2 Flip section D onto the assembled unit, right sides together, matching the first insert's seam lines in sections C and D. Judge the match by eye. Pin exactly on the ¼" (6 mm) seam line, placing the pins parallel to the fabric edges **(fig. 5)**; placing the pins this way mimics the actual seam so you can test the match.

3 Flip D up to check the match. If it's a bit off, flip it back, adjust and re-pin.

4 When you're satisfied with the match, sew the seam, removing the pins as you sew. Press the seams as in Step 3 in the Basic Slice and Insert section at left, and admire your matching skills.

5 When matching two or more intersections, adjust the intersections independently. You may need to adjust one and not the other. The fabric will give a bit, but try not to stretch or pull. Gentle easing will help yield a good match.

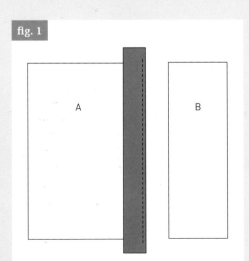

fig. 1

A

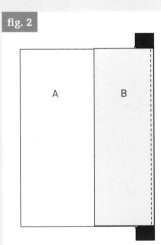

fig. 2

A   B

partial inserts

It's easy to create an insert that isn't continuous from one edge of the block to another, and it's a great way to add complexity and interest to your design.

Make a block with perpendicular inserts. Slice the block vertically where you want the insert to end, as shown by the dotted line in **fig. 6**. Slice section E horizontally where the new insert will appear **(fig. 7)**.

Sew the insert into section E and press the seams. Sew sections E and F back together, carefully matching the horizontal insert sections. Trim the edges of section E to match section F at top and bottom.

An alternative technique for creating partial inserts is simply to slice a square with inserts, rotate one section 180 degrees, and reattach **(fig. 8)**.

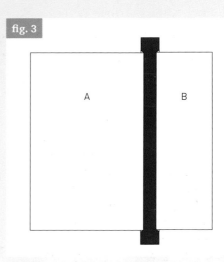

fig. 3

A   B

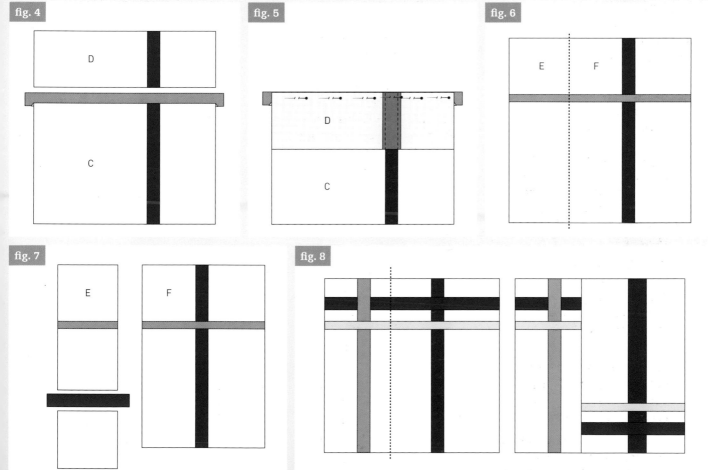

fig. 4

D

C

fig. 5

D

C

fig. 6

E   F

fig. 7

E

F

fig. 8

floating inserts

Creating an insert that appears to float in the background is as easy as adding background fabric to both ends of the insert strip, as shown in **fig. 9**. If you want only one end of the insert to blend into the background, add background fabric to only one end of the strip **(fig. 10)**.

To sew, decide the length of the strip you'd like to float and cut the strip ½" (1.3 cm) longer than necessary to account for seam allowances. Cut background strips the same width as the insert strip, estimating the lengths to reach the background edges. Sew the background strip(s) to one or both ends of the contrasting insert and press the seam. Slice the background fabric and insert the pieced strip.

pointed inserts with diagonal joins

To create diagonal joins for the appearance of pointed inserts, join consistent-width background and contrasting strips at an angle. Position the strips at right angles, right sides together, and sew on the diagonal as shown. Trim the excess fabric, leaving a ¼" (6 mm) seam allowance, and press the seam open **(fig. 11)**.

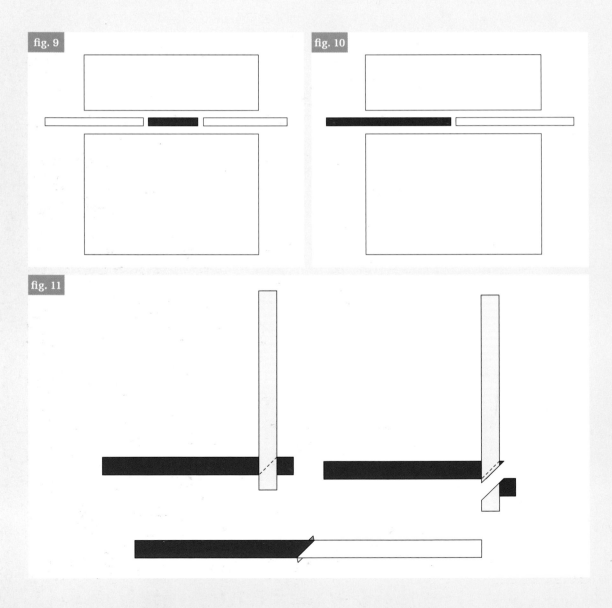

fig. 9

fig. 10

fig. 11

wedge-shaped inserts

Wedge-shaped inserts expand your design possibilities. The Slice and Insert process is the same for wedge-shaped strips except that wedges don't play well together; it's impossible to match seams for two intersecting wedge-shaped strips. To maintain continuous lines, you must intersect a wedge with an even-width strip.

1 Place wedge-shaped strips on the background square and audition their placement **(fig. 12)**. Mark placements with a fabric marker or pins.

2 Insert all the wedges, working on one insert at a time to be sure they don't intersect. Be aware that inserting wedges will skew the background fabric a little more with each insertion.

3 When all the wedges are inserted, insert intersecting consistent-width strips. Again, audition and mark placements and insert one strip at a time **(fig. 13)**. Match seams as directed on page 84 at each intersection. Matching is a little trickier with wedges; be patient and test the matches before you sew.

fig. 12

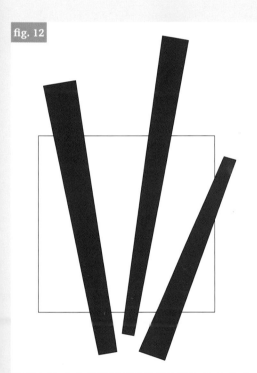

fig. 13

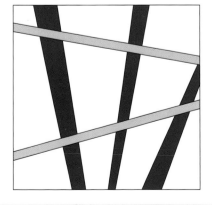

hints and tips

✣ The background fabric will skew as you insert strips, especially when inserting at angles or when using wedges. Start with your background fabric about 2" (5 cm) larger than the finished size of the block.

✣ Keep inserts at least 1½" (3.8 cm) away from the block edges to avoid losing part of the design when squaring up the block.

✣ Cut Slice and Insert blocks apart and combine sections from different blocks to create additional design possibilities.

✣ Using ¾" (2 cm) wide strips will create ¼" (6 mm) wide inserts. This is the smallest strip that we recommend using, and it is the most difficult to work with. Accurate cutting and piecing yield the best results.

✣ For easier slicing and inserting, increase the width of the insert strips.

✣ Have fun with the Slice and Insert technique. For example, try inserting strips that are the same color as the background fabric to create interesting basketweave and plaid designs. Be precise and match seams to create straight lines or forget about matching so the lines appear purposefully disjointed.

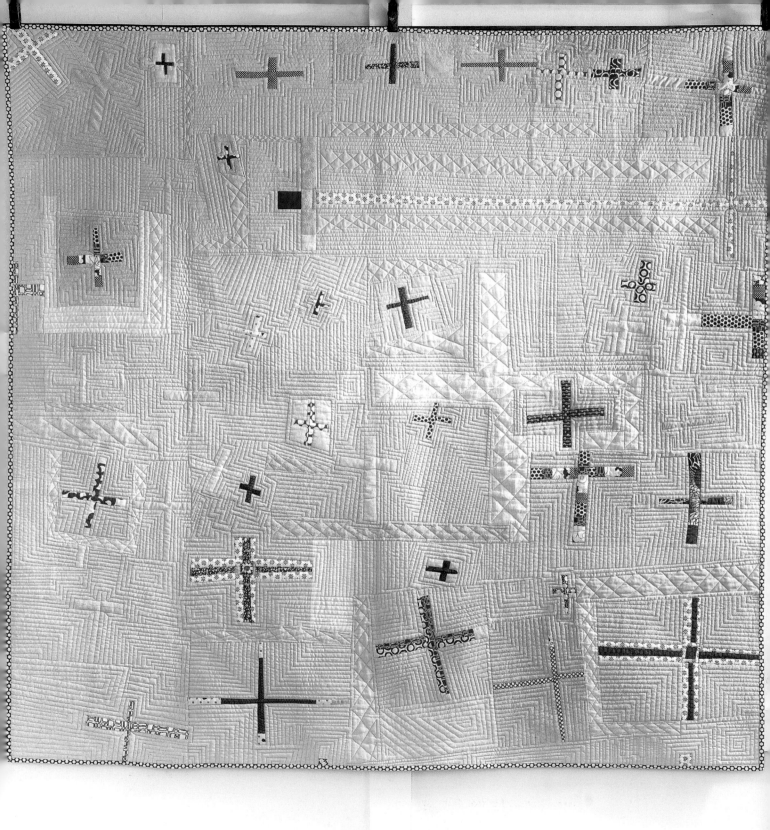

add it up quilt

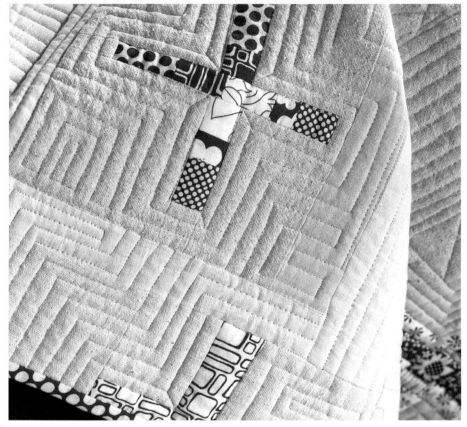

finished size: 62" × 60" (157.5 × 152.5 cm)

The Add It Up quilt is our nod to the traditional cross block and to the quilts that were made during World War I to raise money for the American Red Cross. Add It Up is one of our most improvisational quilts. No two crosses are alike, and partial crosses appear throughout the quilt. Ghost crosses, made from fabric very close in value to the background fabric, hide within the quilt and invite a closer look. The improvisational nature of this quilt makes it challenging to duplicate it exactly, but yours can be similar. Make cross blocks using the variations we describe to give your quilt its own personality.

materials
All fabric amounts are for 45" (114.5 cm) wide fabric.

- 4 yd (3.7 m) beige fabric for background
- ½ yd (45.5 cm) white fabric for ghost crosses
- ¾ yd total of 5 to 8 red small-scale print fabrics
- 4 yd (3.7 m) fabric for backing
- ½ yd (45.5 cm) fabric for binding
- 70" × 68" (178 × 172.5 cm) low-loft cotton batting

tools
- Modern quilter's toolbox (page 10)
- *Optional: Square rulers of varying sizes*

cut the fabric

✂ From background fabric, cut:

- ➤ 11 squares 6½" × 6½" (16.5 × 16.5 cm)
- ➤ 11 squares 9½" × 9½" (24 × 24 cm)
- ➤ 10 squares 12½" × 12½" (31.5 × 31.5 cm)
- ➤ 1 rectangle 11" × 36" (28 × 91.5 cm).

✂ From binding fabric, cut 7 strips 2¼" (5.5 cm) × width of fabric.

✂ From backing fabric, cut two 70" (178 cm) lengths.

construct the quilt

Note: Unless otherwise indicated, all seam allowances are ¼" (6 mm) and are pressed open.

1 Gather the background squares and rectangle and the red and white fabrics near your cutting mat. Cut strips from the red and white fabrics as needed for inserts.

2 Using the Slice and Insert technique, insert two intersecting strips of fabric to construct a basic cross **(fig. 1)**. Change strip width, strip colors, or the position or angle of the strips to create variations.

3 To make a floating cross **(fig. 2)**, cut a strip of red fabric about the size you'd like to float. Add background fabric to each end so it measures a bit longer than the background square. See the instructions on page 86 to complete the block.

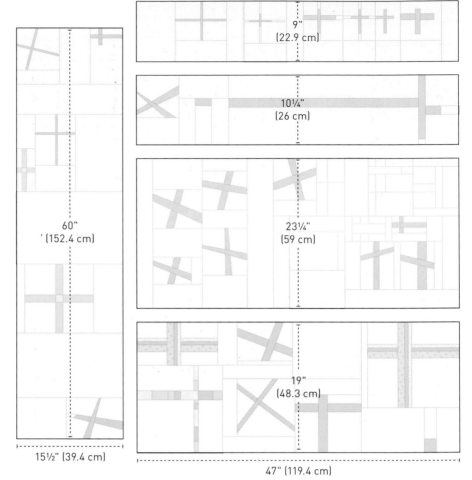

Panel measurements are prior to joining the panels.

Add It Up construction diagram

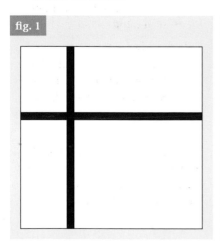

fig. 1

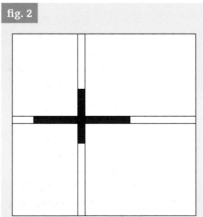

fig. 2

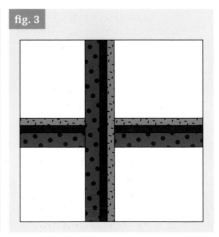

fig. 3

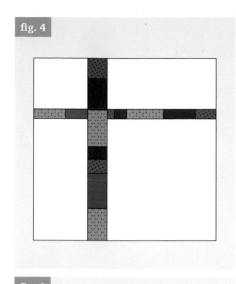

fig. 4

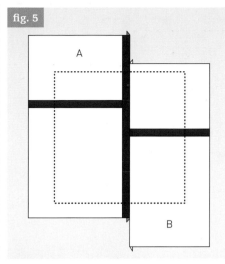

fig. 5

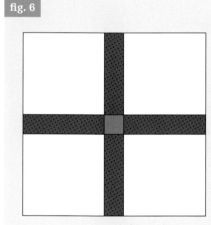

fig. 6

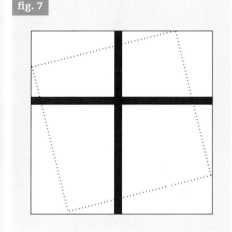

fig. 7

9 Make several ghost crosses for the quilt by replacing the red strips with white fabric.

10 Make a total of thirty-three cross blocks for the quilt. Square all blocks to their largest possible size for flexibility in design. Because your cross blocks will differ from ours, you will need to improvise the setting of your quilt.

11 The Add It Up construction diagram on page 90 shows how we created five panels on the design wall, placed our blocks in the panels, and then filled in with background fabric. Follow our structure or create your own. You can add additional details in the panels by replacing plain background fabric with pieced sections that appear as parts of crosses.

12 Trim the selvedges from the backing fabric. Sew the pieces together along one long edge using a ½" (1.3 cm) seam and press.

13 Make a quilt sandwich from the backing, batting, and quilt top. Baste the layers together.

14 Quilt as desired. Trim the backing and batting to match the quilt top.

15 Join the binding strips to make a continuous length. Bind the raw edges to finish the quilt. See chapter 4 (page 32) for further instructions on basting and binding.

The Add It Up quilt is densely quilted with mathematical symbols across the quilt, moving it further from its traditional cross roots. ✛

4 To make a strip-pieced cross **(fig. 3)**, cut three or more strips from the red fabrics. Choose fabrics that contrast in value or scale to provide definition within the strip set. Create the strip set using the strip-piecing technique (page 116). Cut sections from the strip set to use as inserts.

5 To make a "little bits" cross **(fig. 4)**, sew scraps together and cut straight or angled strips to make the pieced arms of the cross.

6 To make a cross with offset arms, instead of matching the halves of the intersecting strip, move section B down a few inches to offset the arms

(fig. 5). Sew A and B back together as shown and trim to a square.

7 To make a center-focus cross **(fig. 6)**, cut two print strips and slice one in half. Cut a small square the same width as the strip. Sew the square between the strip halves to make a new insert strip. Insert the unbroken strip, then insert the pieced strip to form a cross.

8 To make a tilted cross, start with a basic cross block larger than needed. Place a square ruler at an angle on the finished block, making sure the block extends beyond all four of the ruler's corners, and trim **(fig. 7)**.

shattered quilt

finished size: 62" × 77" (157.5 × 195.5 cm)

The lines and shapes formed by shards of glass from a broken window provided the starting point for the Shattered quilt. Wedge-shaped and consistent-width inserts combine to create this striking, edgy design. The dark color scheme creates a gritty, masculine feel, while a gray cross-woven background fabric showcases the dramatic black inserts. We added multiple borders to frame and extend the design.

materials

All fabric amounts are for 45" (114.5 cm) wide fabric.

4 yd (3.7 m) of fabric for background

2½ yd (2.3 m) of black fabric

4 yd (3.7 m) fabric for backing

⅝ yd (56 cm) fabric for binding

70" × 85" (178 × 216 cm) low-loft cotton batting

tools

Modern quilter's toolbox (page 10)

Fabric marker

southwestern pillows

finished sizes: 12", 14," and 18" (30.5, 35.5, and 46 cm)

This set of three pillows uses linear designs created with ½" (1.3 cm) inserts. We used the floating insert variation to make some strips appear to float or end abruptly, and we used angled strip ends in the Tumbleweed pillow to create pointed inserts. Fabrics with significant value differences create high contrast between the background fabric and the inserts. We chose a modern graphic print to create a bold statement.

materials
All fabric amounts are for 45" (114.5 cm) wide fabric.

- ½ yd (45.5 cm) cream fabric
- ½ yd (45.5 cm) brown fabric
- ½ yd (45.5 cm) print fabric
- 1 yd (91.5 cm) muslin
- 1 yd (91.5 cm) fabric for pillow backs
- 1 yd (91.5 cm) low-loft cotton batting
- One 9" (23 cm) invisible zipper
- Two 12" to 14" (30.5 to 35.5 cm) invisible zippers
- 3 pillow forms, one each 12" (30.5 cm), 14" (35.5 cm), and 18" (45.5 cm) square

tools
- Modern quilter's toolbox (page 10)
- Zipper foot or invisible zipper foot attachment for sewing machine
- Fabric marker

cut the fabric

⁂ From pillow back fabric, cut:

> ‣ 1 square 13" × 13" (33 × 33 cm) for Diamond Eye
>
> ‣ 1 square 15" × 15" (38 × 38 cm) for Cactus
>
> ‣ 1 square 19" × 19" (48.5 × 48.5 cm) for Tumbleweed.

⁂ From muslin and batting, cut:

> ‣ 1 square 16" × 16" (40.5 × 40.5 cm) for Diamond Eye
>
> ‣ 1 square 18" × 18" (45.5 × 45.5 cm) for Cactus
>
> ‣ 1 square 22" × 22" (56 × 56 cm) for Tumbleweed.

⁂ From brown fabric, cut:

> ‣ 1 rectangle 8" × 10" (20.5 × 25.5 cm) for Cactus
>
> ‣ 1 square 10" × 10" (25.5 × 25.5 cm) for Tumbleweed
>
> ‣ 1 strip 1" (2.5 cm) × width of fabric for Cactus and Tumbleweed extensions
>
> ‣ 2 strips 4" × 13½" (10 × 34.5 cm) for Tumbleweed border
>
> ‣ 2 strips 4" × 20½" (10 × 52 cm) for Tumbleweed border.

⁂ From cream fabric, cut:

> ‣ 1 square 14" × 14" (35.5 × 35.5 cm) for Diamond Eye background
>
> ‣ 2 strips 1½" × 7" (3.8 × 18 cm) for Cactus border
>
> ‣ 2 strips 1½" × 10½" (3.8 cm × 26.5 cm) for Cactus border
>
> ‣ 2 strips 1½" × 8½" (3.8 × 21.5 cm) for Tumbleweed border
>
> ‣ 2 strips 1½" × 10½" (3.8 × 26.5 cm) for Tumbleweed border.

⁂ From print fabric, cut:

> ‣ 4 strips 1" (2.5 cm) by width of fabric
>
> ‣ 2 strips 3½" × 9" (9 × 23 cm) for Cactus border
>
> ‣ 2 strips 4" × 16½" (10 × 42 cm) for Cactus border
>
> ‣ 2 strips 2" × 10½" (5 × 26.5 cm) for Tumbleweed border
>
> ‣ 2 strips 2" × 13½" (5 × 34.5 cm) for Tumbleweed border.

construct the pillow tops

Note: Unless otherwise indicated, all seam allowances are ¼" (6 mm) and are pressed open.

DIAMOND EYE PILLOW

1 Gather the 14" (35.5 cm) cream background square and two 1" (2.5 cm) print fabric strips. Use the Slice and Insert technique and refer to **fig. 1** below while completing Steps 2 through 4.

2 Slice the background square from corner to corner and cut a 22" (56 cm) length of one print strip for strip 1. Insert the strip and press.

3 Slice the background square 3¼" (8.5 cm) below and parallel to Strip 1. Cut a new length of print fabric and insert strip 2.

4 Insert Strips 3 and 4 perpendicular to strips 1 and 2 and 3¼" (8.5 cm) apart, matching the seams.

5 Trim the square to 13" × 13" (33 × 33 cm).

CACTUS PILLOW

1 Gather the brown 8" × 10" (20.5 × 25.5 cm) background rectangle and 1" (2.5 cm) wide strips of print and brown fabrics. Orient the rectangle vertically, with the short sides at bottom and top.

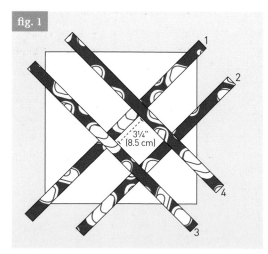

fig. 1

3¼"
(8.5 cm)

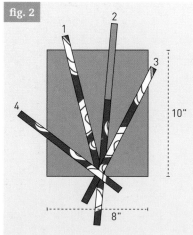

fig. 2

10"

8"

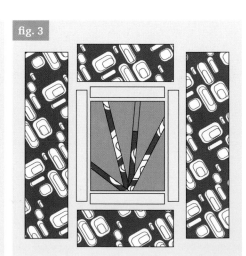

fig. 3

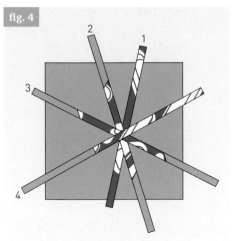

fig. 4

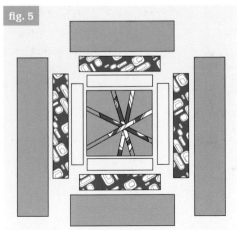

fig. 5

2 Cut two 12" (30.5 cm) and two 10" (25.5 cm) pieces from the print strip. Cut a 6" (15 cm) piece from the brown strip. Sew the 6" (15 cm) brown strip to one end of a 10" (25.5 cm) print strip and press the seam open to make the strip that appears to end in the background.

3 Audition placement of the remaining print strips and mark their locations with pins or a fabric marker. The strips start near the center bottom of the rectangle and run at varying angles.

4 Use the Slice and Insert technique to insert the strips into the background in the order indicated in **fig. 2**.

5 Trim the rectangle to 7" × 8½" (18 × 21.5 cm) to create the pillow's center panel. Add the cream and print borders courthouse-steps style (page 66), one color at a time, adding top and bottom first and then sides **(fig. 3)**; cut slight angles into the borders while piecing, if desired.

6 Trim the assembled unit to 15" (38 cm) square to finish the pillow top.

TUMBLEWEED PILLOW

1 Gather the brown 10" × 10" (25.5 cm) background square and 1" (2.5 cm) wide strips of print and brown fabrics. From the print strip, cut one 12" (30.5 cm), two 7" (18 cm), and one 9" (23 cm) lengths. From the brown fabric strip, cut four 4" (10 cm) and one 6" (15 cm) lengths.

2 Sew a 4" (10 cm) brown strip to each end of the two 7" (18 cm) print strips. To make the inserts pointed, follow the instructions for diagonal joins (page 86). Trim the excess and press.

3 Sew the 6" (15 cm) brown strip to one end of the 9" (23 cm) print strip.

4 Insert the strips in the order indicated in **fig. 4** to achieve a tumbleweed shape. Trim the square to 8½" (21.5 cm) to create the center panel of the pillow.

5 Add the border strips courthouse-steps-style, one color at a time, adding top and bottom first and then sides **(fig. 5)**. Press. Trim slight angles in the borders, Wonky Log Cabin style, if desired.

6 Trim the pillow top to 19" × 19" (48.5 × 48.5 cm)

finishing

1 For each pillow, make a quilt sandwich with a square of muslin, batting, and the pillow top. Baste the layers together with pins.

2 Quilt as desired. Trim the muslin and batting to match the pieced pillow top.

3 After each pillow top is quilted, finish the pillow with backing fabric and an invisible zipper (see page 44).

We quilted each of the pillows with spiraling straight lines echoing the shapes created between the inserts. The quilting lines are ¼" (6 mm) apart.

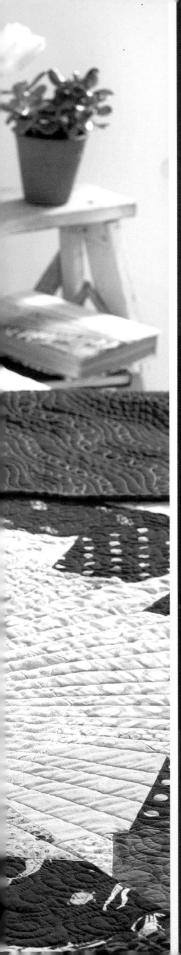

to the point

STITCH AND FLIP TRIANGLE TECHNIQUE AND PROJECTS

Do you cringe a little when a quilt pattern includes triangles because of those bias edges that can stretch and skew? Relax and celebrate the triangle with its sharp points and inherent whimsy! Our improvisational Stitch and Flip Triangle technique gives you all the design momentum of triangles without finicky bias edges. Versatility is the hallmark of the Stitch and Flip Triangle; we used it to create the designs of the three quilts in this section, as well as the sample design ideas that follow in the technique section. Delight in the triangle and imagine what you can do.

◄ Supernova quilt, page 104

stitch and flip triangle technique

To practice this technique and variations, you'll need scraps of fabric, a rotary cutter, cutting mat, acrylic quilter's rulers, squaring rulers to match the finished sizes of your practice blocks, and your sewing machine.

basic stitch and flip triangle square

1 Start with a square of fabric that will become the background to the triangle.

2 Choose a contrasting scrap for the triangle. Scraps can be any shape, but they will need at least one straight sewing edge. Audition the placement angle by laying the scrap across the square, right sides up **(fig. 1)**. Varying the placement angle will result in different triangles in the finished square.

3 While auditioning the placement angle, remember that the dimensions will shrink because of seam allowance; be sure the scrap extends at least ¼" (6 mm) beyond the square's edges at the corner.

4 Flip the scrap right side down, into sewing position, and sew, using a ¼" (6 mm) seam allowance **(fig. 2)**.

5 Align a ruler with the scrap's raw edge and trim the excess background fabric.

6 Flip the scrap right side up and press the seam allowances toward the contrasting fabric. Trim the scrap's edges to square the block and complete the basic Stitch and Flip Triangle square **(fig. 3)**.

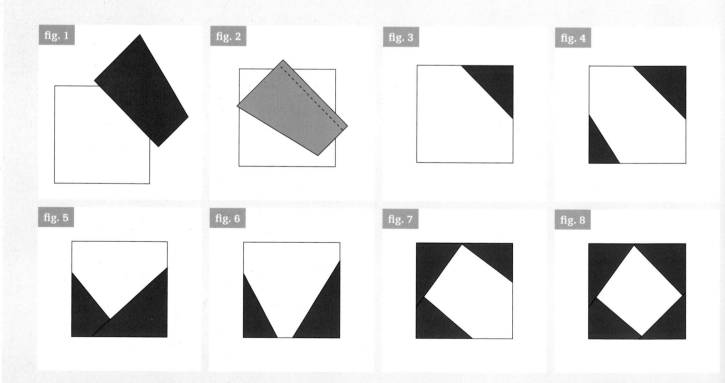

fig. 1 fig. 2 fig. 3 fig. 4

fig. 5 fig. 6 fig. 7 fig. 8

variations

It's easy to create variations on the basic Stitch and Flip Triangle square blocks that can be combined into dynamic patterns.

opposing stitch and flip triangle square

Repeat the Basic Stitch and Flip Triangle square technique to add another triangle to the opposite corner of the square **(fig. 4)**.

spiked stitch and flip triangle square

To the basic square, add a second Stitch and Flip Triangle to an adjacent corner. The triangle bases may **(fig. 5)** or may not **(fig. 6)** overlap each other. This block can serve as the points of a star.

triplet stitch and flip triangle square

Sew Stitch and Flip Triangles to three corners of a square **(fig. 7)**.

four-corner stitch and flip triangle square

Sew Stitch and Flip Triangles to all four sides of a square to reveal a diamond of background fabric **(fig. 8)**. Don't stitch the triangles too close to the center or the background will disappear.

possibilities

Take advantage of the versatility of the Stitch and Flip Triangle square block. At right are some sketches of designs we created with the Stitch and Flip Triangle technique.

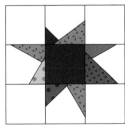

Star

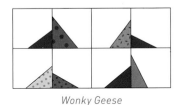

Hourglass

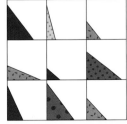

Pennants

Wonky Geese

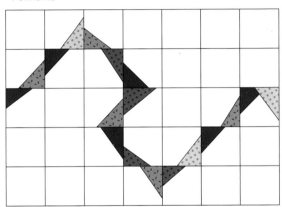

Wandering Zigzag

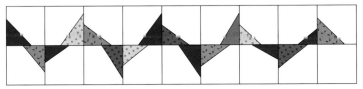

Zigzag

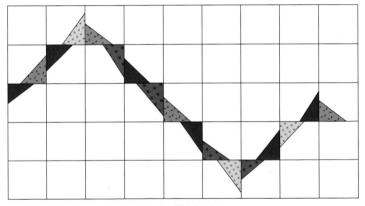

Streak of Lightning

supernova quilt

finished size: 66½" × 78½" (169 × 199.5 cm)

Supernova dazzles with its explosive design and vibrant color palette. Random fragments spin off this medallion-based quilt, generating movement, energy, and excitement. Rich plum and intense mustard create an exuberant feel and high contrast against the light linen background.

materials

All fabric amounts are for 45" (114.5 cm) wide fabric.

- 4 yd (3.7 m) background fabric
- 2¼ yd (2.1 m) total of 8 plum print fabrics
- 1⅔ yd (152.5 cm) total of 6 mustard print fabrics
- 4⅞ yd (4.5 m) fabric for backing
- ⅝ yd (57 cm) fabric for binding
- 74½" × 86½" (189 × 220 cm) low-loft cotton batting

tools

- Modern quilter's toolbox (page 10)
- *Optional: 6½" (16.5 cm) squaring ruler*

cut the fabric

⚹ From background fabric:

  ‣ Cut 18 strips 6½" (16.5 cm) × width of fabric

  ‣ Cross-cut the strips into 102 squares 6½" × 6½" (16.5 × 16.5 cm).

⚹ From plum print fabrics, cut 24 squares 6½" × 6½" (16.5 × 16.5 cm).

⚹ From mustard print fabrics, cut 17 squares 6½" × 6½" (16.5 × 16.5 cm).

⚹ Cut the remaining background, plum print, and mustard print fabrics into 6½" (16.5 cm) strips. Cut pieces from the strips as needed to use as Stitch and Flip Triangles. You can use trimmings to construct triangles as well.

⚹ Cut backing fabric into two 86½" (220 cm) lengths.

⚹ From binding fabric, cut 8 strips 2¼" (5.5 cm) × width of fabric.

construct the quilt

Notes: All seam allowances are ¼" (6 mm) unless otherwise indicated. Press seams in the Stitch and Flip triangles to the side. Press other seams open unless otherwise indicated. This quilt uses the Basic Stitch and Flip Triangle square and the Opposing, Triplet, Spiked, and Four Corner variations (see page 103).

1 Using the background-fabric squares as bases, make Stitch and Flip Triangle squares using the color placement and variations shown in **fig. 1**. The number beneath each image indicates how many of that type of square to make.

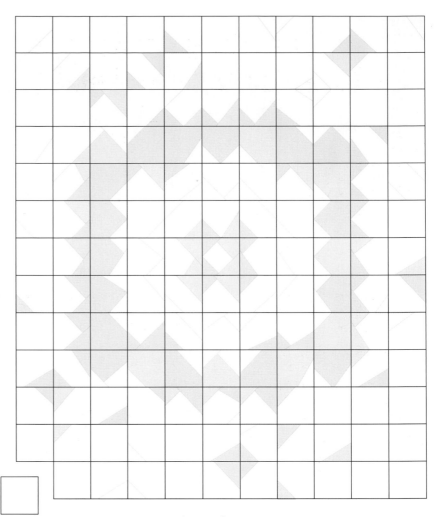

Each block measures 6½" (16.5 cm) square before blocks are joined.

Supernova construction diagram

2 Using a plum print square for each base, make Stitch and Flip Triangle squares using the color placement and variations shown in **fig. 2**. Again, the number beneath each image indicates how many of that type of square to make.

3 Using mustard print squares as the bases, make Stitch and Flip Triangle squares using the color placement and variations shown in **fig. 3**.

4 Use the construction diagram above to arrange the Stitch and Flip Triangles and the remaining background squares on your design wall. Start at the center and work toward the edges of the quilt.

5 When all the blocks are in position, sew each row of blocks together. Replace each completed row on the design wall in its correct position.

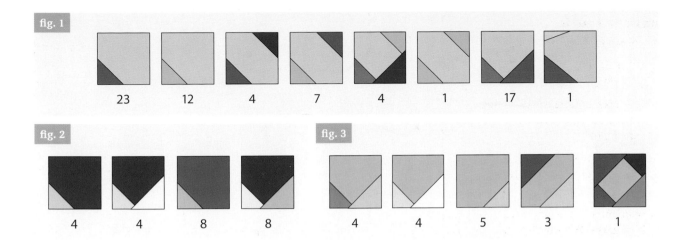

fig. 1

23   12   4   7   4   1   17   1

fig. 2   fig. 3

4   4   8   8   4   4   5   3   1

6   Sew the rows together in order from top to bottom to complete the quilt top.

7   Trim the selvedges from the backing fabric. Sew the two lengths together along one long edge using a ½" (1.3 cm) seam. Press the seam open.

8   Make a quilt sandwich with the backing, batting, and quilt top. Baste the layers together.

9   Quilt as desired. Trim the backing and batting even with the quilt top.

10 Join the binding strips to make a continuous length. Bind the raw edges to finish the quilt. See chapter 4 (page 32) for further instructions on basting and binding.

The quilting on the Supernova quilt, inspired by the medallion theme and the sea motif of the prints, begins at the center and radiates outward. It extends into the background fabric as organic lines filled with effervescent bubbles. ✦

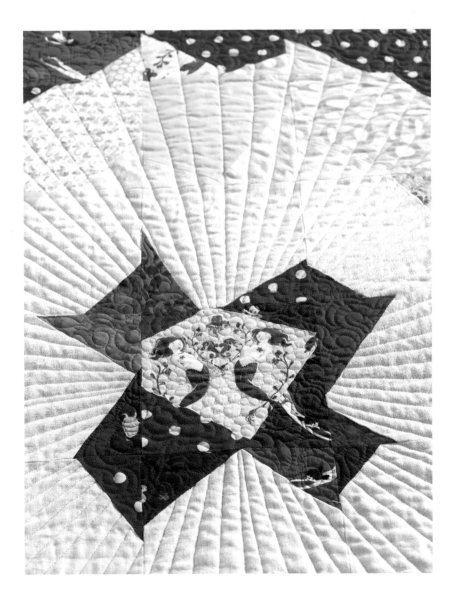

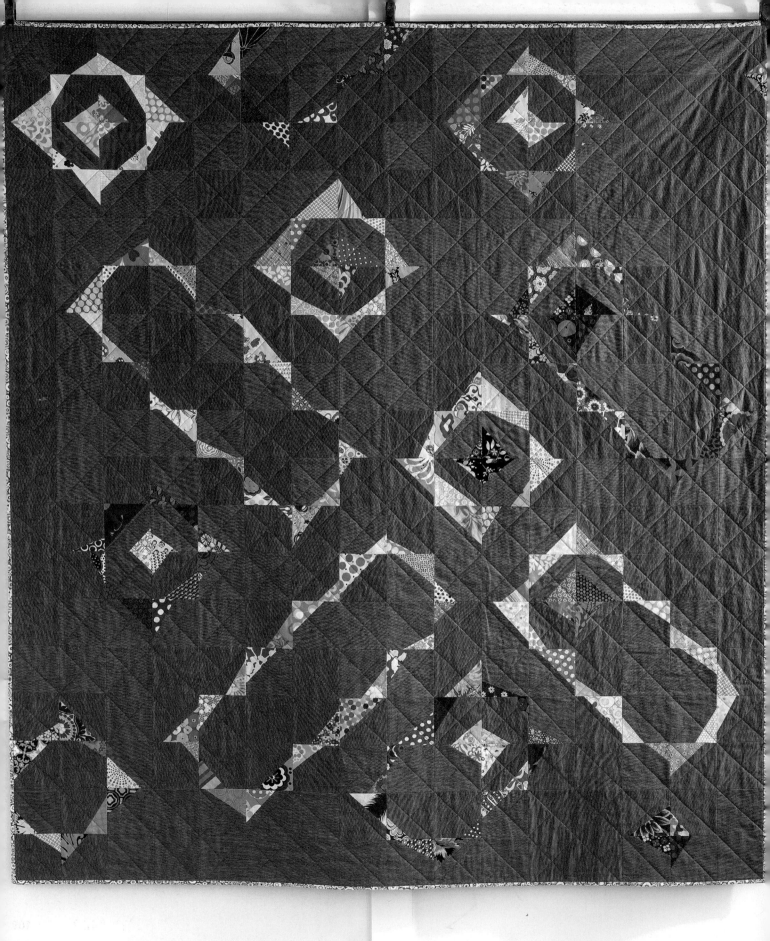

blind co-pilot quilt

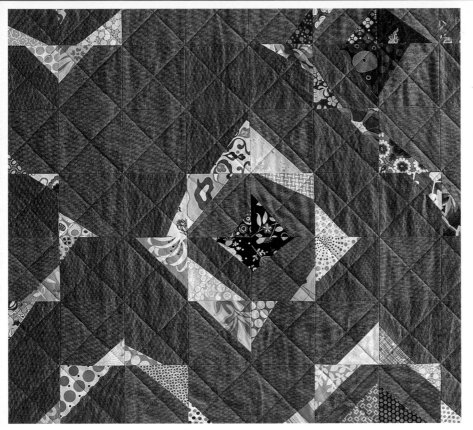

finished size: 64½" × 72" (164 × 183 cm)

Improvisational pieced triangles twirl with bursts of color in the Blind Co-pilot quilt. This design evolved with Stitch and Flip Triangle squares on the design wall as we discovered how to create the dots, diamonds, and rectangles that appear in this quilt. The random triangle tips on the shapes create movement throughout the quilt; they almost seem to spin, as incomplete shapes run off the edge to extend the movement.

materials
All fabric amounts are for 45" (114.5 cm) wide fabric.

- 2 yd (183 cm) total of scraps in the colors listed on page 110
- 4¼ yd (4 m) fabric for background
- 4 yd (3.7 m) fabric for backing
- 72½" × 80" (184 × 203 cm) low-loft cotton batting
- ⅝ yd (57 cm) fabric for binding

tools
- Modern quilter's toolbox (page 10)
- 4½" (11.5 cm) squaring ruler

cut the fabric

⌗ From background fabric, cut 32 strips 4½" (11.5 cm) × width of fabric.

  ➤ Cross-cut the strips into 288 squares 4½" × 4½" (11.5 × 11.5 cm). Set 95 of the background squares aside.

⌗ Collect quantities of 2½" × 4" (6.5 × 10 cm) or larger scraps in each color according to the color chart below.

⌗ From backing fabric, cut two 72" (183 cm) lengths.

⌗ From binding fabric, cut 8 strips 2¼" (5.5 cm) × width of fabric.

construct the quilt

Note: All seams are ¼" (6 mm) unless otherwise indicated. Seams in the Stitch and Flip Triangles are pressed to the side. All other seams are pressed open unless otherwise indicated.

1 Sort the scrap fabrics by color and value. Set aside four dark blue, three dark pink, four orange, seven teal, four yellow, three light purple, and four light red pieces. Place 193 background squares and the remaining pieces within reach of your sewing machine.

2 Sew a Stitch and Flip Triangle on each background square (page 102). Make 193 Stitch and Flip Triangle squares with these scraps (chain piecing, described on page 21, will speed the process):

  ⌗ 10 dark blue
  ⌗ 12 light blue
  ⌗ 5 dark pink
  ⌗ 20 medium pink
  ⌗ 24 light pink

Each block measures 4½" (11.5 cm) square before blocks are joined.

Blind Co-pilot construction diagram

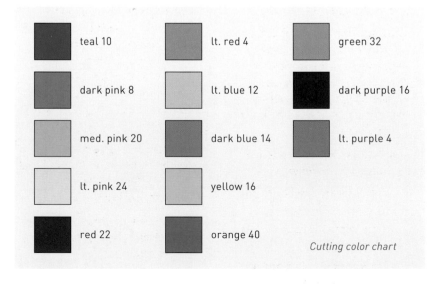

teal 10

dark pink 8

med. pink 20

lt. pink 24

red 22

lt. red 4

lt. blue 12

dark blue 14

yellow 16

orange 40

green 32

dark purple 16

lt. purple 4

Cutting color chart

- ✳ 16 dark purple
- ✳ 36 orange
- ✳ 32 green
- ✳ 3 teal
- ✳ 22 red
- ✳ 12 yellow
- ✳ 1 light purple.

3 Add an additional triangle to twenty-nine of the basic triangle squares to make opposing triangle squares (page 103), using the set-aside scraps and following the color list below.

- ✳ On 3 medium pinks, add a dark pink triangle.
- ✳ On 4 yellows, add a yellow triangle.
- ✳ On 4 light blues, add a dark blue triangle.
- ✳ On 3 dark purples, add a light purple triangle.

- ✳ On 4 oranges, add an orange triangle.
- ✳ On 7 greens, add a teal triangle.
- ✳ On 4 reds, add a light red triangle.

4 Use the construction diagram on page 110 to position the finished triangle squares and ninety-five background squares. Step back and rearrange for a pleasing distribution of sizes, prints, and values.

5 Sew the blocks together in each row, in order, from left to right. Replace each completed row on the design wall in its correct position.

6 Sew rows together from top to bottom to complete the quilt top.

7 Remove the selvedges from the backing fabric. Sew the two lengths together along one long edge, using a ½" (1.3 cm) seam, and press seam open.

8 Make a quilt sandwich from the backing, batting, and quilt top. Baste the layers together.

9 Quilt as desired. Trim the backing and batting to match the quilt top.

10 Join the binding strips to make a continuous length. Bind the raw edges to finish the quilt. See chapter 4 (page 32) for further instructions on basting and binding.

We quilted the Blind Co-pilot quilt with a simple crosshatch bisecting each block, adding to the triangular feel of the quilt. ✣

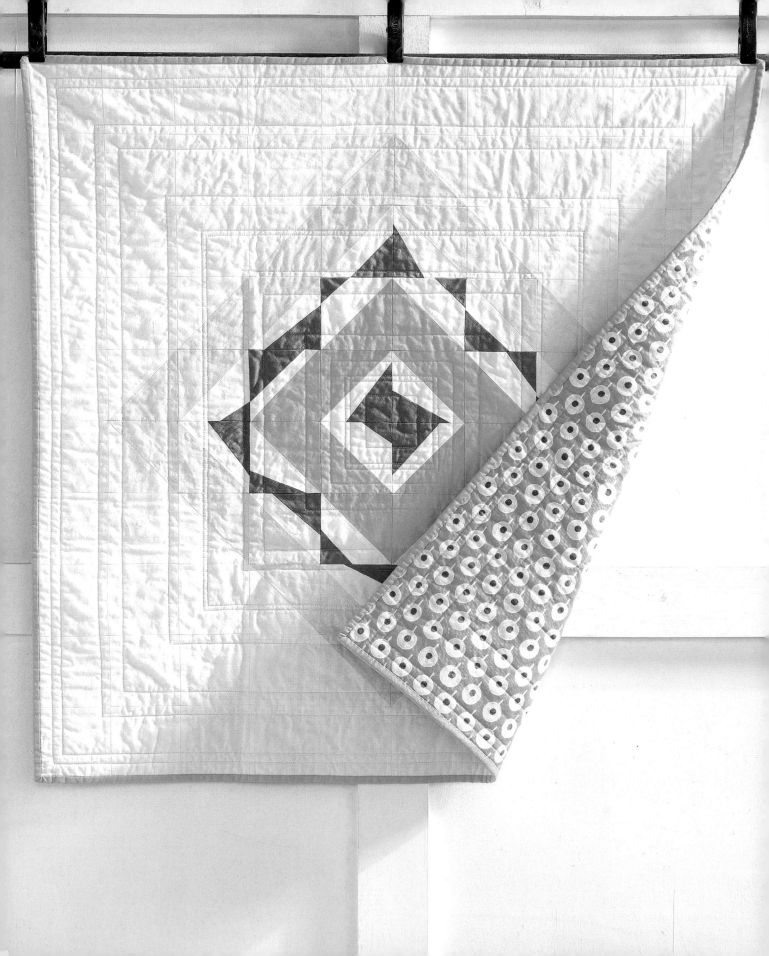

swirling medallion quilt

finished size: 35" × 35" (89 × 89 cm)

Snuggle your little one in the stroller-sized Swirling Medallion quilt, a project that adds another dimension to the Stitch and Flip Triangle square technique. Merging a traditional half-square triangle with an improvisational Stitch and Flip Triangle creates a dynamic new block full of movement and whimsy.

materials
All fabric amounts are for 45" (114.5 cm) wide fabric.

- 1¼ yd (114.5 cm) solid white fabric
- ¼ yd (23 cm) solid turquoise fabric
- ⅓ yd (30.5 cm) solid citron fabric
- ½ yd (45.5 cm) solid gray fabric
- 1¼ yd (114.5 cm) fabric for backing
- 43" × 43" (109 × 109 cm) low-loft cotton batting
- ⅓ yd (30.5 cm) fabric for binding

tools
- Modern quilter's toolbox (page 10)
- *Optional: 4" (10 cm) squaring ruler*

cut the fabric

⁂ From white fabric, cut:

→ 3 strips 4½" (11.5 cm) × width of fabric. Cross-cut these into 20 squares 4½" × 4½" (11.5 × 11.5 cm).

→ 6 strips 4" (10 cm) × width of fabric. Cross-cut these into 60 squares 4" × 4" (10 × 10 cm).

⁂ From turquoise fabric, cut 1 strip 4½" (11.5 cm) × width of fabric. Cross-cut this strip into 6 squares 4½" × 4½" (11.5 × 11.5 cm).

⁂ From citron fabric, cut 2 strips 4½" (11.5 cm) × width of fabric. Cross-cut these into 14 squares 4½" × 4½" (11.5 × 11.5 cm).

⁂ From gray fabric, cut 4 strips 4" (10 cm) × width of fabric. Cross-cut these into 24 randomly sized rectangles between 3" (7.5 cm) and 6" (15 cm) long.

⁂ From binding fabric, cut 4 strips 2¼" (5.5 cm) × width of fabric.

construct the quilt

Note: All seams are ¼" (6 mm) unless otherwise indicated. Press seams in the Stitch and Flip triangles to the side. Press all other seams open unless otherwise indicated.

1 To construct the half-square triangles, pair each of the twenty colored 4½" (11.5 cm) squares with a 4½" (11.5 cm) white square, right sides together, aligning the edges. Draw a diagonal line from corner to corner on the top square in each pair.

2 Chain-piece the pairs (see page 21), sewing ¼" (6 mm) away from the line. Take the chain back to the machine and

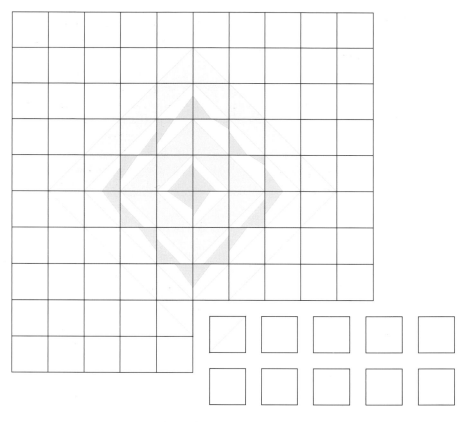

Each block measures 4" (10 cm) square before blocks are joined.

Swirling Medallion construction diagram

sew ¼" (6 mm) from the line on the opposite side **(fig. 1)**.

3 Take the blocks to the ironing board and set each seam with a brief press. Snip the blocks apart.

4 Cut each block in half along the drawn line to make two half-square triangles. Press the seams. Trim sixteen citron-white half-square triangles to measure 4" × 4" (10 × 10 cm), with the seam running diagonally from corner to corner, and set them aside.

5 Take twelve each of the turquoise-white and citron-

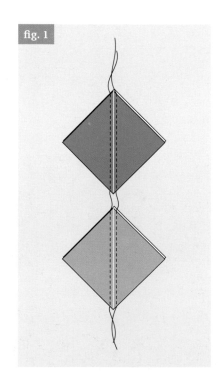

fig. 1

fig. 2

white half-square triangles and the random-sized gray rectangles to the sewing machine. Follow the instructions for basic Stitch and Flip Triangles on page 102 to add gray Stitch and Flip Triangles to the white side of each half-square triangle, making twenty-four blocks **(fig. 2)**.

6 Use a rotary cutter and square ruler to trim the blocks to 4" (10 cm) square, making sure the original seam line runs from corner to corner.

7 Starting at the center, arrange the twelve turquoise/white/gray Stitch and Flip blocks, then add the twelve citron/white/gray blocks, referring to the construction diagram on page 114. Make adjustments in block placement so adjacent triangles overlap as often as possible, aiming for a continuous line of gray triangles.

8 Complete the medallion with the sixteen citron/white half-square triangles. Finish the top by adding sixty white background squares.

9 Sew the top row of blocks, right sides together, from left to right to construct the row. Repeat for all ten rows, replacing each row on the design wall when it is complete.

10 Sew the rows together in order from top to bottom, right sides together, matching seams and aligning raw edges. Press.

11 Press the backing fabric. Create a quilt sandwich with the backing, batting, and quilt top. Baste.

12 Quilt as desired. Trim the backing and batting to match the quilt top.

13 Join the binding strips to make a continuous length. Bind the raw edges to finish the quilt. See chapter 4 (page 32) for further instructions on basting and binding.

We quilted Swirling Medallion with concentric squares that radiate out to the edges of the quilt.

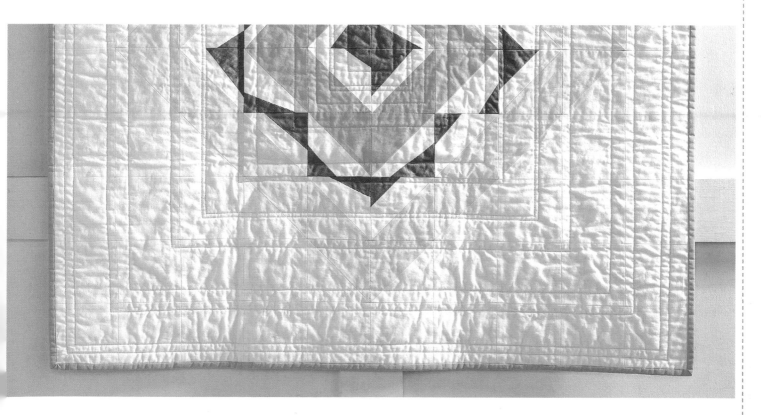

strip tease

STRIP-PIECING
TECHNIQUE AND PROJECTS

Sewing long strips of fabric together, then recutting
and resewing the strips to create intricate designs,
characterizes the patchwork of the Seminole Indians of
Florida. The technique is called strip piecing, in which
strips of fabric are cut and joined lengthwise to resemble
striped fabric. The quilt design determines the size
and number of strips. Cut strip sets, or sewn units of
strips, perpendicular to the seam lines or at angles to
form blocks, shapes, or pieced strips to integrate into
your quilts. Faster and easier than piecing individual
scraps, strip piecing is a versatile way to create modern
patchwork for modern quilts.

◀ Fiesta wall quilt, page 122

strip-piecing technique

Strip piecing is a versatile technique. Complex designs can be achieved with relatively simple piecing. Make some simple strip sets, start cutting, and experiment on your design wall. To practice the basic strip-piecing technique and variations, you'll need some generous scraps or pieces of fabric, a rotary cutter, cutting mat, acrylic quilter's rulers, pins, and of course, your sewing machine and design wall.

basic strip piecing

Basic strip piecing begins with cutting the fabrics into strips, then sewing the strips together. Follow these instructions and you'll have strip piecing down in no time and can move on to all the applications of this easy technique.

1 Fold the fabric in half lengthwise, matching the selvedges. Fold the fabric in half again, aligning the fold with the selvedges. Place the folded fabric on the cutting mat, aligning the fold with a horizontal line on the mat. Trim the right edge of the fabric square with the fold **(fig. 1)**. Rotate the entire cutting mat, with the fabric still in place, to position the fabric for further cuts without disturbing the folds and squared edge. *Note:* **Figs. 1–3** show the ruler and fabric in position for a right-handed person to square the fabric end. Left-handed users may find it helpful to view the illustration in a mirror.

2 To cut a consistent-width strip, align a horizontal ruler line with the fold and cut the strip, using the ruler markings to gauge the strip width **(fig. 2)**. For best results, cut the strips in half at the center fold to yield shorter strips, which are easier to strip piece. We like to work with strips no longer than 22" (56 cm). With longer strips, it's more challenging to maintain a straight strip set.

3 Gather the strips and begin placing them alongside each other on your design wall. Pay attention to value as you arrange the strips. Step back and see how the strips interact. Work with them on the design wall until you are satisfied with the arrangement.

4 We teach the pairing method to strip piece: we sew strips into pairs, then sew pairs together, and the pairing continues until we've joined all the strips. We find that this method yields a straight, even strip set. To begin, take the strips off the design wall one pair at a time, placing each pair right sides together. Stack the pairs, taking care to keep them in order. To remember the positions of the strips on the design wall, place a pin on the first pair or take a snapshot for reference.

5 If you have difficulty keeping edges aligned when sewing, pin the strip pairs together every 3" (7.5 cm). Reduce the stitch length on the sewing machine to 2.0 mm; shorter stitches keep seams from coming apart when the strips are recut.

6 Chain sew the pairs (see page 21) using a ¼" (6 mm) seam allowance, keeping the raw edges aligned.

7 Take the chain of paired strips to the ironing board, keeping the pairs connected. Press on the seam line to set the seam and then press each pair's seam open. Pressing seams open helps keep the strips straight, without curving or distortion, while pressing to the side tends to skew the strips, eventually causing the

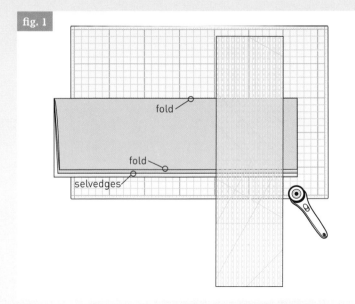

fig. 1

fold

fold

selvedges

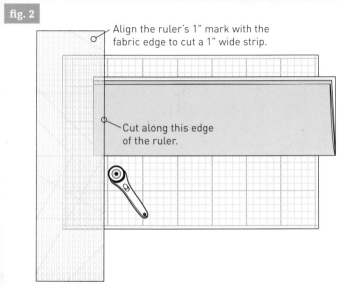

fig. 2

Align the ruler's 1" mark with the fabric edge to cut a 1" wide strip.

Cut along this edge of the ruler.

fig. 3

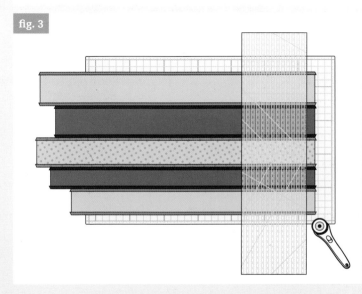

strip set to curve. However, when joining strips less than 1" (2.5 cm) wide, carefully press the seams to the side.

8   Place the pressed strip pairs back on the design wall in order, starting with the pair with the pin. Snip them apart as you place them on the wall.

9   Use the same process to stitch the sewn pairs together, making sets of four strips. Remove the pairs from the design wall two by two, place them right sides together, make a stack and take them to the sewing machine. Make sure the pin is still in the first set so you can remember its position on the design wall.

10   Chain sew the strip pairs together and again press seams open. Replace these strip sets in order on the design wall, snipping the chain apart as you go. Repeat this process until you have all the strips sewn into one large strip set.

11   Place the completed strip set on your cutting mat, wrong side up, with the seams running left to right. (With the seam allowances facing up, the strip set is more stable for more accurate cutting.) Square one end of the strip set to prepare for cross-cutting the strips. Depending on the final design you may cut straight or angled strips or larger shapes to use as blocks (fig. 3).

alternate method

For strip sets with just a few strips or short strips, it's easier to sew strips one at a time. When using this method, reverse sewing direction with each strip as shown in **fig. 4** to keep the strip set from distorting. Sew strip 1 to strip 2 from top to bottom and add strip 3 by sewing from bottom to top. Strip 4 is joined from top to bottom. Press the seams open after each strip addition. Continue in this pattern to maintain a straight strip set.

string blocks

Strip piecing can also be done on a foundation. This is commonly referred to as string piecing, named after the strings, or long strips of fabric, used to create the blocks.

1 Start with a foundation square of muslin or paper. We prefer paper since it can be removed and is light and inexpensive. Reduce the stitch length on your machine to 1.5 for paper piecing.

2 Choose a string a bit longer than the diagonal of the square and place it right side up along the center diagonal of the foundation. Secure with a dab of glue. Place the next string on the first, right sides together, aligning the raw edges. Sew with a ¼" (6 mm) seam allowance **(fig. 5)**.

3 Flip the second string right side up and press. Continue adding strings in this manner to cover one side of the foundation **(fig. 6)**. Start again at the center and add strings to cover the other half of the foundation square. Strings can also be applied from corner to corner (rather than from the center outward) or starting at any diagonal on the square.

4 When the foundation square is covered with strings, lay the square, foundation side up, on the cutting mat and trim, using the foundation as a template. Remove the paper to complete the block.

fig. 4

fig. 5

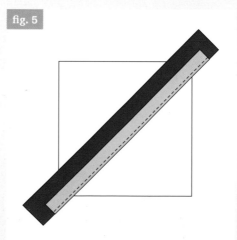

fig. 6

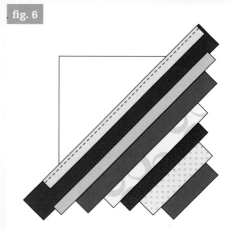

hints and tips

✤ Use recycled computer paper or pages from telephone
   books as foundation papers for string piecing.

✤ To make the foundation papers easier to remove, fold
   them along the seam lines.

✤ To avoid curving of strip sets, sew strips using the
   pairing method or reverse the sewing direction as you
   sew one strip at a time.

✤ Consider value as you create strip sets. Different values
   placed side by side will create contrast.

fiesta wall quilt

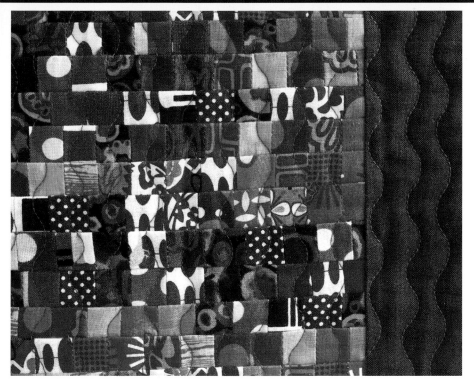

finished size: 24" × 24" (61 × 61 cm)

A color-blocked strip-pieced square is the focus of this stunning wall quilt. The Fiesta quilt takes advantage of strip piecing to create an intricate center square that becomes the focal point of the design. The strips are grouped to create bands of color within the square. We included a few prints with white backgrounds to create light within the square, making the piece almost sparkle. The strip-pieced square is then bordered with three rings of solid color and bound in deep purple to create a dramatic frame.

materials
All fabric amounts are for 45" (114.5 cm) wide fabric.

- 3" to 5" (7.5 to 12.5 cm) × 22" (56 cm) each of 20 to 25 print fabrics in equal proportions of orange, pink-red, and purple
- ⅜ yd (34.5 cm) purple solid fabric
- ¼ yd (23 cm) dark orange solid fabric
- ⅜ yd (34.5 cm) medium orange solid fabric
- 32" × 32" (81.5 × 81.5 cm) low-loft cotton batting
- 1 yd (91.5 cm) fabric for backing
- ¼ yd (23 cm) fabric for binding

tools
- Modern quilter's toolbox (page 10)
- Seam ripper

cut the fabric

* Cut 30 strips from the print fabrics, each 1" × 22" (2.5 × 56 cm), cutting about a third of the strips from each color family.

* From purple fabric, cut:
  > 1 strip 10½" × 5" (26.5 × 12.5 cm)
  > 1 strip 10½" × 2" (26.5 × 5 cm)
  > 2 strips 16½" × 3½" (42 × 9 cm)

* From dark orange fabric, cut:
  > 1 strip 16½" × 3½" (42 × 9 cm)
  > 1 strip 16½" × 1½" (42 × 3.8 cm)
  > 2 strips 20½" × 2½" (52 × 6.5 cm).

* From medium orange fabric, cut:
  > 1 strip 20½" × 3½" (52 × 9 cm)
  > 1 strip 20½" × 1½" (52 × 3.8 cm)
  > 2 strips 24½" × 2½" (62 × 6.5 cm).

* From backing fabric, cut 1 square 32" × 32" (81.5 × 81.5 cm).

* From binding fabric, cut 3 strips 2¼" (5.5 cm) × width of fabric.

construct the quilt

Note: Unless otherwise indicated, all seam allowances are ¼" (6 mm) and are pressed open.

1 Gather the 1" (2.5 cm) strips and place them on the design wall. Arrange them in bands of color until you have a pleasing distribution. If you want one color to dominate, use more bands of that color or concentrate it in a single area. Use from three to seven strips in a single-color band **(fig. 1)**.

2 Sew the strips together using the pairing method on page 118. Press. Trim the strip set to 15½" × 22" (39.5 × 56 cm).

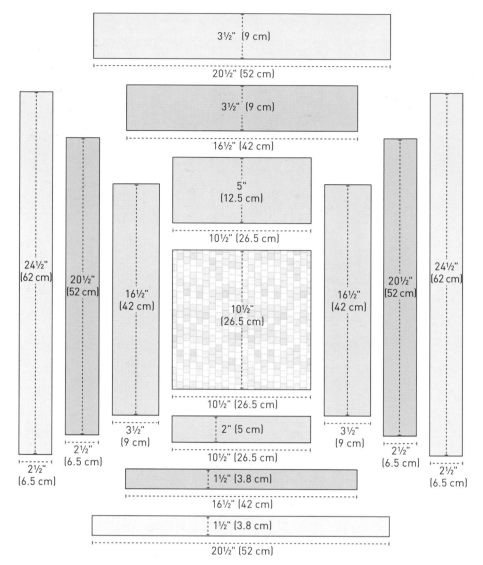

Measurements are prior to joining the sections.

Fiesta construction diagram

3 Place the completed strip set on the cutting mat, wrong side up, with the seams parallel to the bottom of the cutting mat. Cut a straight edge on one end of the strip set with a rotary cutter and ruler **(fig. 2)**.

4 Cut as many 1" (2.5 cm) strips as possible from the strip set. You may get as many as twenty-one strips.

5 Place two pieces of tape horizontally on the design

wall about 11½" (29 cm) apart. Arrange the strip-pieced strips between the tapes to begin creating the square. Stagger the strips so that bands of color are placed as desired and similar fabrics aren't aligned **(fig. 3)**.

6 Use a seam ripper to remove portions of a strip that fall outside the taped area and move each portion to the opposite end of its strip to

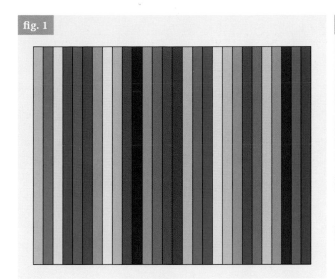

fig. 1

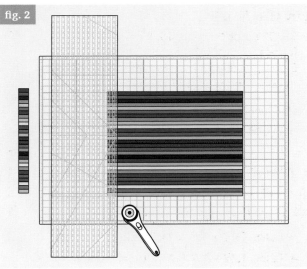

fig. 2

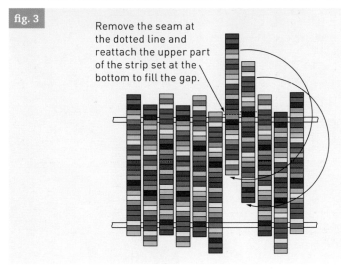

fig. 3

Remove the seam at the dotted line and reattach the upper part of the strip set at the bottom to fill the gap.

fill in blank spaces. Sew the partial strips together to make whole strips.

7 When the area is completely filled, sew the strips together in order. Use the pairing method. Replace pairs on the design wall in order and continue pairing and sewing until the strip-pieced section measures at least 10½" (26.5 cm) wide. Don't worry about matching seams; it won't matter one bit.

8 Press the seams to the side. The strips will be much more stable now, but be sure to press by lifting the iron rather than sliding it back and forth. Press all the seams in the same direction.

9 Place the strip-pieced section wrong side up on the cutting board. Square and trim the section to measure 10½" × 10½" (26.5 × 26.5 cm). This is the center panel of the quilt.

10 Add the borders one color at a time, sewing the top and bottom pieces first and then the sides. The purple border is first, then dark orange, then light orange, as shown in the construction diagram on page 124. On the inner border, press the seam allowances toward the purple fabric. On outer borders, press seams open.

11 Make a quilt sandwich with the backing fabric, batting, and quilt top. Baste the layers together.

12 Quilt as desired. Trim the batting and backing to match the quilt top.

13 Join the binding strips to make a continuous length. Bind the raw edges to finish the quilt. See chapter 4 (page 32) for further instructions on basting and binding.

Fiesta is quilted with the wavy lines of a serpentine stitch; rows of stitching are about ⅜" (1 cm) apart.

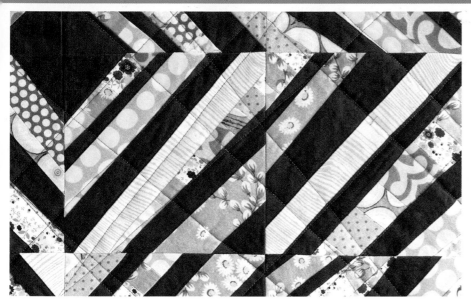

Fractured quilt

finished size: 36½" × 48½" (92.5 × 123 cm)

The baby quilt goes modern. The Fractured quilt is a dramatic design combining strip piecing and string-pieced blocks (string blocks are a foundation-pieced version of strip piecing described on page 120). The design radiates from the upper left, with the "fracture" formed by solid purple triangles in the corners of four blocks coming together. Strategically placed solid purple strips within the string-pieced blocks form a radiating design that creates the illusion of fractured glass. For visual texture, we used strip-pieced strips as some of the strings in the blocks.

materials

All fabric amounts are for 45" (114.5 cm) wide fabric. Fabrics labeled 45" wide may be narrower after removing selvedges, so it's unlikely you'll get a full 44" × 56" (112 × 142 cm) backing panel. If the backing is at least 2" to 3" (5 to 7.5 cm) larger than the quilt top on all sides, it can be used with care. If the backing is too narrow, create a pieced backing as detailed on page 35 or buy twice as much fabric and piece the backing from two equal-length panels.

- 2 yd (183 cm) solid dark purple fabric
- ⅓ yd (30.5 cm) each of 8 print fabrics in greens and purples
- 44½" × 56½" (112 × 142 cm) low-loft cotton batting
- 1⅝ yd (149 cm) fabric for backing
- ⅜ yd (34.5 cm) fabric for binding
- 48 squares of lightweight paper, 6½" × 6½" (16.5 × 16.5 cm)

tools

- Modern quilter's toolbox (page 10)
- 6½" (16.5 cm) squaring ruler
- Acid-free glue stick

cut the fabric

* Cut 1 strip from each of the 8 print fabrics, ranging from 1" to 3" (2.5 to 7.5 cm) × width of fabric, then cross-cut each strip in half.

* From the binding fabric, cut 5 strips 2¼" (5.5 cm) × width of fabric.

construct the quilt

Note: Unless otherwise indicated, all seams are ¼" (6 mm). Press seams in the foundation piecing to the side. Press all other seams open.

1   Place four 6½" (16.5 cm) paper squares on the cutting mat. Cut one 3" (7.5 cm) strip from the purple fabric. Cut four random triangles from the strip and place one on the inner corner of each square **(fig. 1)**. Use a dab of glue stick to attach the triangles to the paper foundations. We'll refer to these as center fracture squares; set them aside for now. Use the remainder of the purple strip as strings for piecing other blocks.

2   Create two different strip sets using the sixteen print fabric strips, being sure that the sewn strip set measures at least 10" × 20" (25.5 × 51 cm). Straighten one end of each strip set, then cross-cut each set into strips ranging in width from 1" to 2½" (2.5 to 6.5 cm) **(fig. 2)**. We'll refer to these strips as pieced strings in the following steps.

3   Cut strips ranging in width from 1" to 2½" (2.5 to 6.5 cm) from the remainder of the print and purple fabrics to use as strings in the blocks.

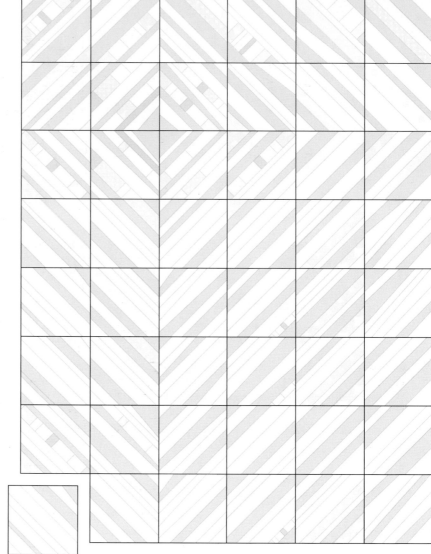

Each block measures 6½" (16.5 cm) square before blocks are joined.
Fractured construction diagram

Make three stacks: the pieced strings, the purple strings, and the print strings.

4   Reduce the machine's stitch length to 1.5 mm for paper piecing. Retrieve the center fracture squares from Step 1. Audition a string on the foundation by lapping it ½" (1.3 cm) over the edge of one square's purple triangle; the string must be long enough to extend beyond the paper edges. Flip the string onto the purple triangle, right sides together, aligning the edges **(fig. 3)**. Sew and press.

5   Flip the string right side up and press into place. Continue attaching strings in this

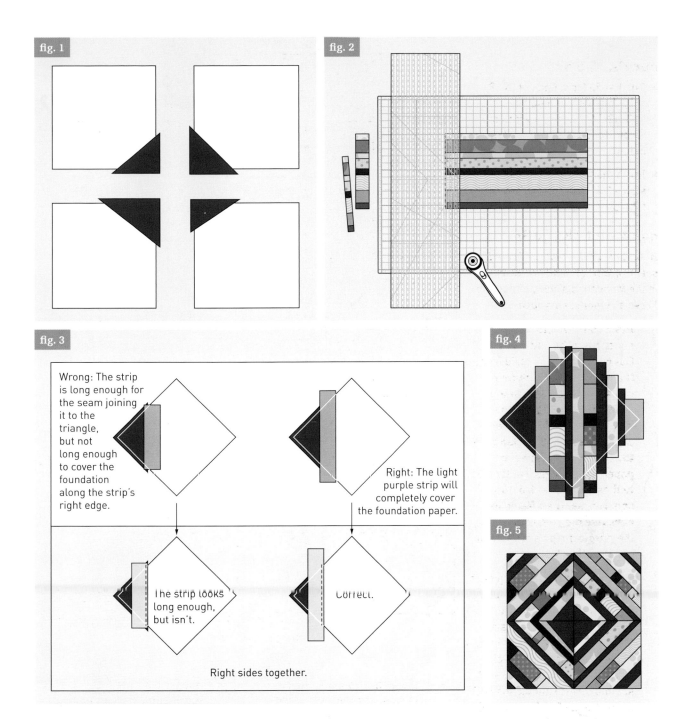

fig. 1

fig. 2

fig. 3

Wrong: The strip is long enough for the seam joining it to the triangle, but not long enough to cover the foundation along the strip's right edge.

Right: The light purple strip will completely cover the foundation paper.

The strip looks long enough, but isn't.

Correct.

Right sides together.

fig. 4

fig. 5

manner until the paper square is covered. Be sure there are at least three solid purple strings in each square **(fig. 4)**.

6 Turn the block over so the foundation paper is on top. Align the 6½" (16.5 cm) square ruler with the foundation

paper and trim the block. Repeat Steps 4 through 6 to make the other three center fracture blocks.

7 The placement of the solid purple strings is important to create the fractured design. As you piece the four center

blocks, roughly align the purple strings to create the fractured look **(fig. 5)**. Place the center blocks on the design wall when complete.

8 The remaining string blocks are constructed a little differently. Place a foundation square alongside the center blocks on the design wall. Lay a purple string diagonally across the foundation paper, right side up, roughly aligning it with a purple string in the adjacent block. Secure the string with a dab of glue. At the machine, add strings to the foundation from the purple strip to one corner, then sew strings from the first purple string to the opposite corner of the foundation paper **(fig. 6)**. The strings should extend at least ¼" (6 mm) beyond the paper.

9 Be sure that there are at least three purple strings in each string block. Determine the placement of the first purple strip for each block on the design wall and form somewhat continuous lines with the purple strips as they move from block to block. For best results, work on adjacent blocks at the same time so that you can judge the position of each purple string by eye **(fig. 7)**.

10 When all forty-eight blocks are complete, carefully remove the foundation papers and replace the blocks, in order, on the design wall. Refer to the construction diagram on page 128.

11 Adjust your sewing machine stitch length for regular sewing. Join the blocks in order from left to right to create rows, returning completed rows to the design wall.

12 Sew the rows together from top to bottom. Pin at block seam intersections, right sides together, matching block seams and aligning edges. Sew and press to complete the quilt top.

13 Make a quilt sandwich with the backing fabric, batting, and quilt top. Baste the layers together.

14 Quilt as desired. Trim the backing and batting to match the quilt top.

15 Sew the binding strips together to make a continuous length. Bind the raw edges to finish the quilt. See chapter 4 (page 32) for further instructions on basting and binding.

We quilted Fractured with randomly placed straight lines to reinforce the energetic drama of the geometric piecing. ✛

fig. 6

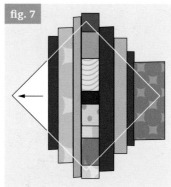

fig. 7

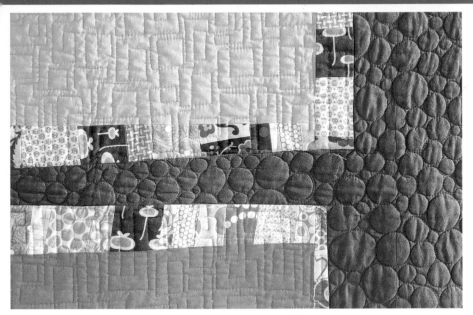

stepping-stones quilt

finished size: 64" × 72" (162.5 cm × 183 cm)

Have you ever peeked between houses in the city and spied a few moss-covered stones, almost buried, but still visible? A stone pathway leading to a hidden backyard garden inspired the design of the Stepping-Stones quilt. The stones are colorful rectangles surrounded by angled strip piecing. We used beautiful galvanized shot cottons to bring a special radiance to the quilt.

materials
All fabric amounts are for 45" (114.5 cm) wide fabric except where indicated.

- 3½ yd (3.2 m) fabric for background
- Fat quarters (18" × 22" [45.5 × 56 cm] fabric pieces) of 8 different prints in blues and greens (if fat quarters are unavailable, purchase ¼ yd (23 cm) pieces and cut the strips in half)
- ½ yd (45.5 cm) green fabric
- ½ yd (45.5 cm) dark turquoise fabric
- ½ yd (45.5 cm) medium turquoise fabric
- ¼ yd (23 cm) light turquoise fabric
- 4⅛ yd (3.8 m) fabric for backing
- ⅝ yd (57 cm) of fabric for binding
- 72" × 80" (183 × 203 cm) low-loft cotton batting

tools
- Modern quilter's toolbox (page 10)
- 48" (122 cm) ruler

cut the fabric

Note: Label the "stones" 1 through 7 with a sticky note or pinned scrap of paper as you cut.

⁎ From background fabric, cut:

➤ 2 strips 9" (23 cm) × width of fabric (A)

➤ 2 strips 19" (48.5 cm) × width of fabric (B)

➤ 4 strips 4" (10 cm) × width of fabric (C)

➤ 1 strip 6" (15 cm) × width of fabric (D)

➤ 1 strip 8" (20.5 cm) × width of fabric (E).

➤ Cut remaining background fabric as needed to extend the stones.

⁎ From green fabric, cut:

➤ 1 piece 6" × 21" (15 × 53.5 cm) (stone 7)

➤ 1 piece 8" × 4½" (20.5 × 11.5 cm) (stone 3)

➤ 1 piece 8" × 22" (20.5 × 56 cm) (stone 2).

⁎ From dark turquoise fabric, cut:

➤ 1 piece 1½" × 11" (3.8 × 28 cm) (stone 6)

➤ 1 piece 9" × 26½" (23 × 67.5 cm) (stone 1).

⁎ From medium turquoise fabric, cut:

➤ 1 piece 8" × 26" (20.5 × 66 cm) (stone 5).

⁎ From light turquoise fabric, cut:

➤ 1 piece 6" × 23" (15 × 58.5 cm) (stone 4)

➤ 1 piece 4½" × 4½" (11.5 × 11.5 cm) (stone 8).

⁎ From the 8 print fat quarters, cut 40 strips ranging from 1½" to 3½" (3.8 to 9 cm) × 22" (56 cm).

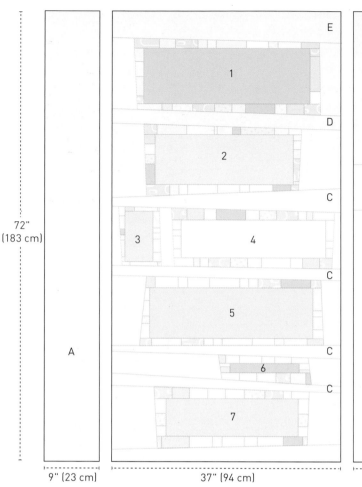

Panel measurements are prior to joining panels.

Stepping-Stones construction diagram

⁎ From the binding fabric, cut 8 strips 2¼" (5.5 cm) × width of fabric.

⁎ From the backing fabric, cut two 72" (183 cm) lengths.

construct the quilt

Note: Unless otherwise indicated, all seam allowances are ¼" (6 mm) and are pressed open.

1 Use the print strips to construct five different strip sets as described on page 118, with each set containing at least one strip of each print fabric.

2 Cut the five strip sets into consistent-width strip-pieced strips of varying widths.

Cut strips no less than 1½" (3.8 cm) and no more that 4" (10 cm) wide.

3 Sort the strip-pieced strips into stacks by width. This will help you choose the best strip width to add when surrounding the rectangles.

4 Gather the rectangles for stones 1 through 7. Sew strip-pieced strips to two sides of each rectangle. Pin to align edges if necessary. Press.

5 Trim the strip-pieced strips even with the top and bottom of each rectangle **(fig. 1)**. Save the trimmings, sewing them together as necessary to form useful lengths.

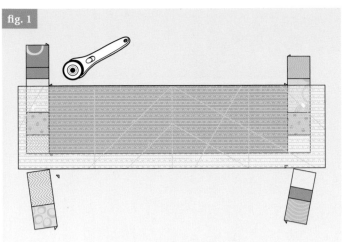

fig. 1

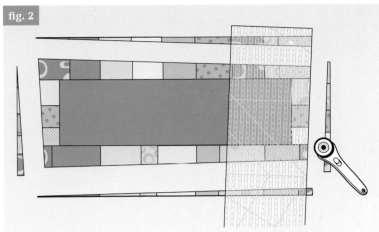

fig. 2

6   Sew strip-pieced strips to the tops and bottoms of the seven rectangles. Join two or more strips of the same width as needed to reach the stone's length. Press. Trim the strip-pieced strips even with the rectangle sides.

7   Use a rotary cutter and ruler to trim the strip piecing at slight angles on all four sides of each rectangle **(fig. 2)**.

8   Add strip-pieced strips to the sides of the stone 8 square, and then to the top and bottom. Do not angle the sides of this stone. Trim stone 8 to the desired size now.

9   The Stepping-Stones quilt consists of three panels, as shown in the construction diagram on page 134. Construct the center panel first. The sizes of your stones may differ from ours.

10   Put two pieces of tape vertically on your design wall, 37" (94 cm) apart. Stagger stones 1 through 7 in order within the taped column.

11   Sew a narrow piece of background fabric between stones 3 and 4, joining them. Adjust the height of the stones

as necessary so the top and bottom edges of the unit are straight.

12   Add background fabric to extend each stone to measure 37" (94 cm) from side to side, treating the 3+4 unit as one stone. Return each 37" (94 cm) unit to the design wall in the correct position as it is completed.

13   Join stones 1 through 7 with background fabric pieces using angle piecing (page 50).

14   Cut a width-of-fabric strip of background fabric wide enough to bring the total length of the center panel to 72" (183 cm), adding extra inches for angle piecing. Sew this strip to the bottom of stone 7 and trim the sides. Square the bottom of the center panel so the entire panel measures 37" × 72" (94 × 183 cm).

15   Sew a strip of background fabric to the left side of stone 8, extending its width to 19" (48.5 cm).

16   Cut a 25" (63.5 cm) piece from one of the B background strips and sew it to the tip of stone 8. Sew the other B strip

to the top of stone 8. Trim this panel to 72" (183 cm); it is the right panel.

17   To make the left panel, sew the two A background strips together and trim to 72" (183 cm). Sew the right and left panels to the center panel to complete the quilt top.

18   Trim the selvedges from the backing fabric. Sew the pieces together along one long edge using a ½" (1.3 cm) seam. Press the seam open.

19   Make a quilt sandwich from the quilt backing, batting, and quilt top. Baste the layers together.

20   Quilt as desired. Trim the backing and batting to match the quilt top.

21   Join the binding strips to make a continuous length. Bind the raw edges to finish the quilt. See chapter 4 (page 32) for further instructions on basting and binding.

The stones are the focal point of this quilt. Angela used a long-arm quilting machine to create a dense geometric design within the stones. The pebble design in the background fabric accentuates its sheen. ✦

GoinG crazy

MODERN CRAZY-PIECING
TECHNIQUE AND PROJECTS

Crazy piecing and crazy quilts have a revered place in quilting history. Traditional crazy quilts are pieced with cloth of varying sizes, types, shapes, and colors; are sewn in random arrangements on a foundation; and are embellished with elaborate embroidery or lace. In our modern version, we maintain the random shapes and arrangement, but leave out the embellishment and the foundation. Modern crazy piecing is a free-flowing, expressive way to work—almost like designing your own fabric. After you've mastered the technique, you'll be able to make crazy-pieced sections to place in quilts, use in pillows, or add to any other project you can imagine.

◀ Winter Windows quilt, page 140

modern crazy-piecing technique

Modern crazy piecing works best with a large number of fabrics. We recommend at least eight. Both large- and small-scale prints work well. Scraps are perfect for crazy piecing. Consider color and value as you experiment with fabrics. Combining darks and lights will provide depth and create movement within the crazy-pieced sections.

To calculate how much fabric you need for a crazy-pieced project, use this formula. One fat quarter, or 18" × 22" (45.5 × 56 cm) piece of fabric, cut into 2" to 3" (5 to 7.5 cm) wide strips, will yield about 144 square inches (930 square cm) of crazy piecing, or a 12" × 12" (30.5 × 30.5 cm) crazy-pieced section.

Gather your rotary cutter, acrylic quilter's rulers, cutting mat, and sewing machine, along with fat quarters in a variety of print fabrics, to try out the basic crazy-piecing technique by following these steps.

basic modern crazy piecing

1 Cut width-of-fabric strips from the fat quarters. Strips can vary in width from about 2" to 3½" (5 to 9 cm). Divide the 22" (56 cm) strips in half (if you cut folded fabric, divide strips by cutting at the fold). Strips may be cut straight or at a variety of angles **(fig. 1)**.

2 When using scraps, choose four-sided scraps with at least one straight edge. Scraps should be at least 2½" (6.5 cm) square because seam allowances will make each piece smaller.

3 Determine a finished size for the crazy-pieced section before you begin. Use the lines on the cutting mat to measure the section as it grows.

4 Pair the strips. Consider color and value as you make the pairs so that there is some contrast between the strips in each pair. If using scraps, pair them in the same way.

5 Sew each pair of strips with right sides together, using a ¼" (6 mm) seam allowance. Press seams open; this is important when crazy piecing to reduce bulk so that pieced sections will lie flat.

6 Cut each strip set into sections as shown in **fig. 2**. Vary the size and angle of the cut sections.

7 To build larger sections, combine pairs to make four-piece blocks or add a scrap to make three-piece blocks. Offset the seams when joining pairs **(fig. 3)**. These are the building blocks of crazy piecing.

8 Continue building the crazy piecing by combining the three- and four-piece blocks.

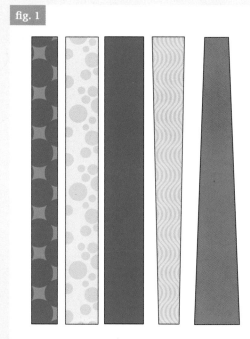

fig. 1

Join pieces at angles to create the "crazy" look. To do this, lay a section on a four-piece block at the desired angle, right sides together **(fig. 4)**.

9 Align a ruler with the edge of the angled section and trim the excess. Sew as indicated using a ¼" (6 mm) seam. Press seam open.

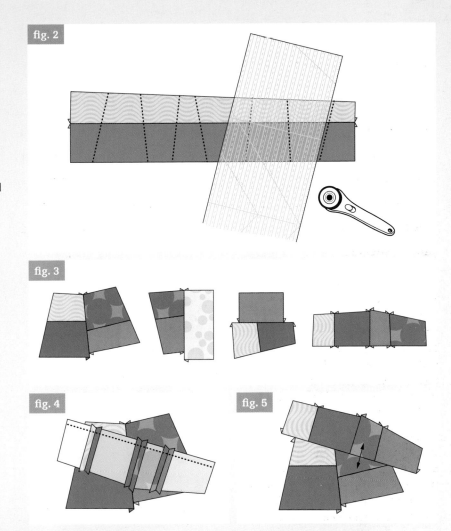

fig. 2

fig. 3

fig. 4

fig. 5

10 Notice in **fig. 5** that identical fabrics meet along the seam line. Similar fabrics across the seam line trick the eye and camouflage where sections are joined; camouflage joins when possible.

11 Continue making three-piece and four-piece units and sewing these together to create a large section of crazy piecing. Remember to press seams open. In no time you'll have a large crazy-pieced unit that you can use whole or cut into smaller pieces to place in projects.

hints and tips

❖ If you get stuck and can't find a good place to make an addition, don't hesitate to make a cut, creating a new edge where you can add a section.

❖ Pay special attention to fabrics that are very dark or very light. They will draw the eye within the crazy piecing.

❖ Place crazy-pieced sections on the design wall every so often. Stand back and take a look so you can see how the fabrics are working together.

❖ Don't throw away trimmings; use them to start new sections or add to others.

❖ Substitute crazy-pieced sections for any piece in your quilts: borders, block centers, sashing, or even a whole quilt.

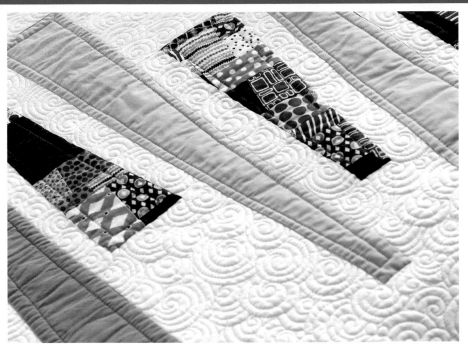

winter windows quilt

finished size: 66½" × 92" (169 × 234 cm)

An elaborate glass window and a gray winter day inspired the Winter Windows quilt. Crazy piecing resembles stained glass, and with this quilt we challenged ourselves to mimic the complex patterns in the glass with fabric. We placed darks and lights in the crazy-pieced sections to draw the eye and create movement in the windows. The muted blue-greens, grays, and creams create the mood of a quiet, still winter day. The large area of negative space provided an opportunity to echo the wedge-shaped windows with quilting.

materials

All fabric amounts are for 45" (114.5 cm) wide fabric.

- 1½ yd (137 cm) total of 10 to 12 print fabrics in mixed values of gray, navy, aqua, black, and white
- 5 yd (4.6 m) of cream solid fabric for background
- ¼ yd (23 cm) medium gray solid
- ½ yd (45.5cm) light gray solid
- ½ yd (45.5 cm) light green solid
- ¼ yd (23 cm) aqua solid
- 5 yd (4.6 m) fabric for backing
- ⅔ yd (61 cm) fabric for binding
- 74½" × 100" (189 × 254 cm) low-loft cotton batting

tools

- Modern quilter's toolbox (page 10)

cut the fabric

❋ From background fabric, cut:

> ‣ 2 strips 30" (76 cm) × width of fabric

> ‣ 2 strips 25" (63.5 cm) × width of fabric

> ‣ 1 strip 2" (5 cm) × width of fabric

> ‣ 1 strip 4" (10 cm) × width of fabric

> ‣ 1 strip 6" (15 cm) × width of fabric.

❋ Cut the print fabrics into strips 2" (5 cm), 2½" (6.5 cm), or 3" (7.5 cm) × width of fabric. Strips can be cut a consistent width or at angles. Cut the strips in half (if you've cut the fabric while folded, simply cut at the center fold).

❋ From backing fabric, cut:

> ‣ 1 piece 42" × 100" (106.5 × 254 cm) (A)

> ‣ 2 pieces 30" × 40" (76 × 101.5 cm) (B)

> ‣ 1 piece 22" × 30" (56 × 76 cm) (C).

❋ From binding fabric, cut 9 strips 2¼" (5.5 cm) × width of fabric.

construct the quilt

Note: Unless otherwise indicated, all seam allowances are ¼" (6 mm) and are pressed open.

1 Pair the print strips, considering value so that each pair has some contrast. Sew pairs together using a ¼" (6 mm) seam allowance.

2 Using the Modern Crazy-Piecing technique on page 136, make nine crazy-pieced sections, each 5½" × 12½" (14 × 31.5 cm). Cut each of these

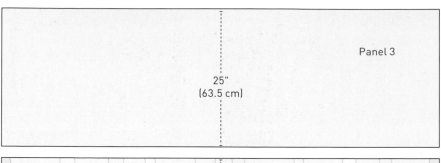

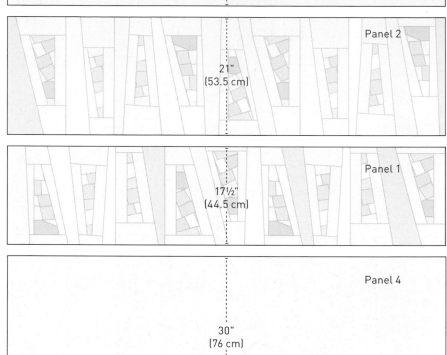

Panel measurements are prior to joining the panels. The width of the quilt is flexible.

Winter Windows construction diagram

sections from top to bottom at an angle into two wedge shapes **(fig. 1)**, for a total of eighteen wedges. Improvise as you cut the wedges so no two will be alike. The short edge of each wedge should be at least 1½" (3.8 cm) wide.

3 From the 2" (5 cm), 4" (10 cm), and 6" (15 cm) wide strips of cream background fabric, cut pieces to surround each

crazy-pieced wedge, cutting additional strips as needed. Sew two strips to the sides of each wedge, right sides together. Press. Trim the background strips even with the top and bottom of the wedge **(fig. 2)**.

4 Add strips to the top and bottom of each wedge to create wedge blocks. To make the crazy-pieced wedges

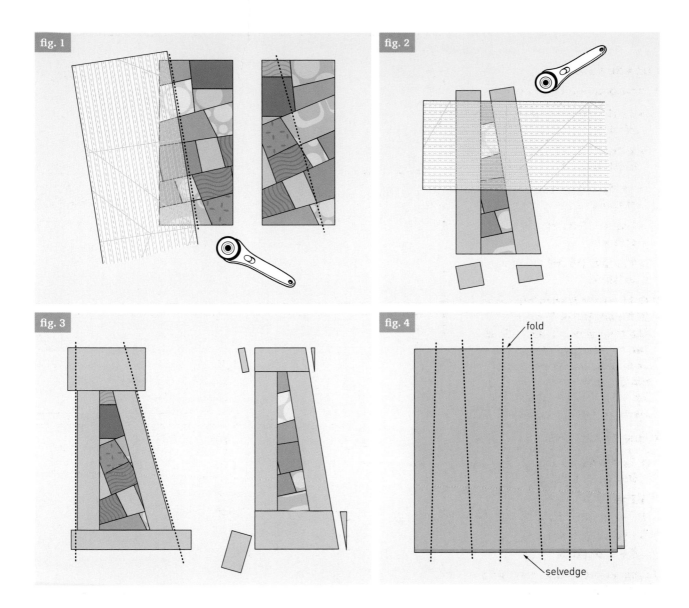

appear staggered in the panels, make these strips different widths. Make nine wedge blocks 22" (56 cm) tall and nine wedge blocks 19" (48.5 cm) tall. Trim strips even with the sides of the block **(fig. 3)**.

5 Fold each piece of solid-color fabric in half lengthwise, matching selvedges. Cut wedge shapes at least 2½" (6.5 cm) wide at the narrow end and 3½" (9 cm) at the wide

end from the fabrics. Angles can be gentle or dramatic. Position the initial cut near the edge of the fabric and then cut additional wedge shapes side by side. Divide each piece at the fold to create two wedges **(fig. 4)**. Cut three aqua wedges, four medium gray wedges, six light gray wedges, and six light green wedges.

6 Place the colored wedges and crazy-pieced wedge blocks on the design wall to make two

horizontal panels. Alternate wedge blocks with colored wedges as shown in the construction diagram on page 142. Use the 19" (48.5 cm) wedge blocks for panel 1 and the 22" (56 cm) wedge blocks for panel 2.

7 To construct the panels, sew the wedge blocks and colored wedges together one at a time from left to right, right sides together. Sew the first three wedges together, alternating

the narrow and wide ends. If the right edge of the sewn section slants to the left, add the next wedge with its wide end at the top. If it slants to the right, add the next wedge with the narrow end at the top. As you sew the wedges together, try to keep the bottom edges of the wedge blocks aligned **(fig. 5)**.

8 Complete panel 1 and trim to 17½" (44.5 cm) high, using a rotary cutter, ruler and cutting mat to square up the panel. Measure the final length of panel 1.

9 Repeat Steps 7 through 9 to make panel 2. Measure panel 2 and trim or add additional wedges so that panel 1 and 2 are the same length. Trim panel 2 to 21" (53.5 cm) high.

10 Sew the 30" (76.2 cm) wide pieces of cream background fabric together along their short ends to make one long strip. Cut the length equal to the side-to-side measurement of panels 1 and 2. Repeat with the 25" (63.5 cm) pieces. Sew panels 1 through 4 together according to the construction diagram on page 142 to finish the quilt top.

11 Sew the three smaller backing pieces together along the short edges using ½" (1.3 cm) seam allowances and press. Sew this unit to the largest backing piece along the long edges, creating a 71" × 100"

(180 × 254 cm) backing (if your quilt's width is different, adjust accordingly).

12 Make a quilt sandwich from the backing, batting, and quilt top. Baste the layers together.

13 Quilt as desired. Trim the backing and batting to match the quilt top.

14 Join the binding strips to make a continuous length. Bind the raw edges to finish the quilt. See chapter 4 (page 32) for further instructions on basting and binding.

The quilting on the Winter Windows quilt echoes the wedges in the pieced sections of the quilt. Swirls fill the background to create a beautiful texture. ✛

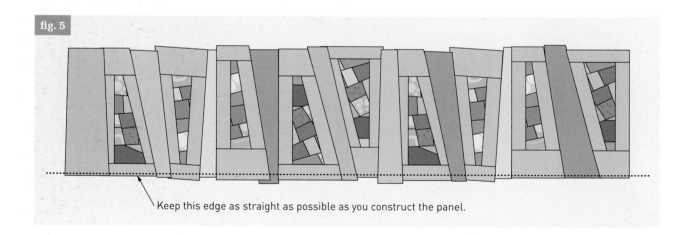

fig. 5

Keep this edge as straight as possible as you construct the panel.

blue ice quilt

finished size: 54½" × 72½" (138.5 × 184 cm)

Can you feel the chill? Turquoise, blue, gray, and winter white come together in this cool yet invigorating quilt. A cloudless blue sky over a frozen pond on a brisk winter day inspired the color and design of this quilt. The intricate look of crazy piecing suits this design. The angles and irregular shapes in the crazy piecing mimic cracks that form within the ice. Angular crazy-pieced centers and skewed strips in the Log Cabin blocks create additional hard edges in this modern quilt.

materials
All fabric amounts are for 45" (114.5 cm) wide fabric.

- 1¼ yd (114.5 cm) total of 8 to 10 turquoise, blue, and gray prints in a mix of values
- 2 yd (1.8 m) of turquoise fabric
- 2 yd (1.8 m) of cream fabric
- 2 yd (1.8 m) of light gray fabric
- 3½ yd (3.2 m) of fabric for backing
- ½ yd (45.5 cm) fabric for binding
- 62½" × 80½" (159 × 204.5 cm) low-loft cotton batting

tools
- Modern quilter's toolbox (page 10)

cut the fabric

✴ From the print fabrics, cut strips 2" (5 cm), 2½" (6.5 cm), or 3" (7.5 cm) × width of fabric. Strips can be cut a consistent width or at angles. Cut each strip in half to yield a 22" (56 cm) length (approximate).

✴ From the turquoise, gray, and cream fabrics, cut strips as needed. Strips can range in width from 1" (2.5 cm) to any width.

✴ From the binding fabric, cut 7 strips 2¼" (5.5 cm) × width of fabric.

✴ From the backing fabric, cut 2 lengths each 62" (157.5 cm) long.

construct the quilt

Note: Unless otherwise indicated, all seam allowances are ¼" (6 mm) and are pressed open.

1 Review the basic Modern Crazy Piecing technique beginning on page 136. Pair the print strips, considering value so that each pair has some contrast. Sew strip pairs together and press.

2 Use the sewn strips to make the following crazy-pieced sections:

  ✴ Three sections 8" × 16" (20.5 × 40.5 cm)

  ✴ One section 8" × 14" (20.5 × 35.5 cm)

  ✴ One section 6" × 10" (15 × 25.5 cm).

3 Cut two rectangular shapes from each of the four 8" (20.5 cm) crazy-pieced sections and one from the 6" (15 cm) section, for a total of nine pieced shapes to become the centers of nine Elongated

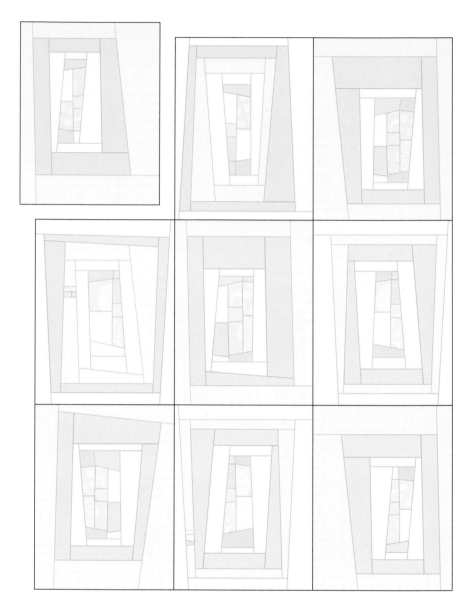

Each block measures 18½" × 24½" (47 × 62 cm) before blocks are joined.

Blue Ice construction diagram

Wonky Log Cabin blocks (see page 69). Centers of varying sizes add interest and charm to the quilt.

4 Using painter's tape, make a 19" × 25" (48.5 × 63.5 cm) rectangle on the design wall. Gather turquoise, gray, and cream strips and the nine crazy-pieced centers. Cut additional strips as needed.

5 Some logs in our Wonky Log Cabin blocks have tiny inserts of leftover crazy piecing. Before sewing these log strips into a block, slice the solid strip and insert the scrap of leftover crazy piecing. Trim the edges of the crazy piecing even with the strip **(fig. 1)**.

6 Make five Elongated Wonky Log Cabin blocks, each 18" × 24" (45.5 × 61 cm) finished. Make the first round of logs in cream, the second round in turquoise, and the final round of logs in gray **(fig. 2)**. Add one round of logs at a time. Press the first round of seam allowances away from the crazy piecing, but press the remaining seam allowances open. After adding the first two rounds, place the block within the taped rectangle.

7 Measure from the edge of the block to the tape to estimate the strip widths for the final round of logs. Trim the block to 18½" × 24½" (47 × 62 cm) to complete.

7 Make four more blocks, this time with four rounds of logs **(fig. 3)**. The first and final round of logs are cream; make the other two rounds whatever color you choose. Use the taped rectangle to help determine the widths of the final strips to create an 18½" × 24½" (47 × 62 cm) block.

8 Arrange the nine completed blocks on the design wall according to the construction diagram on page 148, alternating the blocks by the color of the final round of logs.

9 Sew the blocks in each row together in order and replace the rows on the design wall as they are completed. Sew the rows together in order from top to bottom, pinning to align the raw edges and match seams.

10 Trim the selvedges from the backing fabric. Sew the sections along one long edge with a ½" (1.3 cm) seam and press.

11 Make a quilt sandwich with the backing, batting, and quilt top. Baste the layers together.

12 Quilt as desired. Trim the backing and batting to match the quilt top.

13 Join the binding strips to make a continuous length. Bind the raw edges to finish the quilt. See chapter 4 (page 32) for further instructions on basting and binding.

We quilted the Blue Ice quilt with straight lines spaced ½" (1.3 cm) apart in an angular pattern across the quilt. The quilting emphasizes the cool, sharp qualities of the quilt. ✛

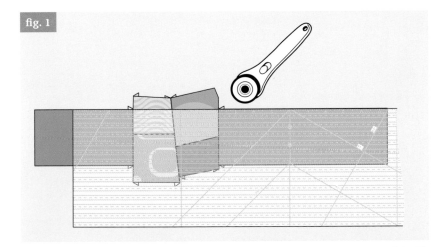

fig. 1

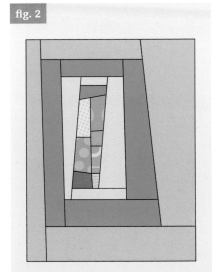

fig. 2

fig. 3

crazy placemats

finished size: each placemat is 14" × 19" (35.5 × 48.5 cm)

These placemats are a terrific way to give crazy piecing a try and use up loads of scraps. We created the placemat designs by arranging different sizes and shapes of crazy-pieced sections within the background. Experiment with shapes and placement to create your own designs. We like it when the crazy piecing has presence on the placemat. In other words, don't make your crazy-pieced sections too small.

materials
*All fabric amounts are for 45" (114.5 cm) wide fabric.
These amounts will make four placemats.*

- 1¼ yd (114.5 cm) total of 8 to 10 blue and green print fabrics in a mix of values
- 2 yd (183 cm) beige fabric for background
- 1 yd (91.5 cm) fabric for backing
- ⅝ yd (57 cm) fabric for binding
- 1 yd (91.5 cm) of 45" (114.5 cm) wide low-loft cotton batting

tools
- Modern quilter's toolbox (page 10)

cut the fabric

❋ Cut the print fabrics into strips 2" (5 cm), 2½" (6.5 cm), or 3" (7.5 cm) × width of fabric. Strips can be cut a consistent width or at angles. Cut the strips in half (if you've cut the fabric folded, simply cut at the center fold).

❋ From binding fabric, cut 8 strips 2¼" (5.5 cm) × width of fabric.

construct the placemats

Note: Unless otherwise indicated, all seam allowances are ¼" (6 mm) and are pressed open.

1   Pair the print fabric strips, considering value so that each pair has some contrast. Sew the strip pairs together and press.

2   Using the basic Modern Crazy Piecing technique (page 136), make four crazy-pieced sections, each 12" × 12" (30.5 × 30.5 cm).

3   Cut each completed crazy-pieced section into interesting shapes in various sizes. You can cut squares and rectangles or cut irregular shapes as we did. **Fig. 1** shows how one 12" × 12" (30.5 × 30.5 cm) section of crazy piecing was cut to create the shapes for one placemat.

4   On your design wall, use blue painter's tape to mark a 15" × 20" (38 × 51 cm) rectangle. This rectangle will help you audition the placement of the crazy-pieced shapes and plan the pieces of background fabric to be added around the crazy piecing. Work on one placemat at a time. **Fig. 2** shows how we placed our crazy-pieced shapes.

5   After deciding on a placement, place a pin in the design wall at each corner of each crazy-pieced shape; the pins will allow you to return the shapes to their positions on the design wall.

6   Have the background fabric ready for cutting and cut background strips as needed. Working from the design wall, estimate the length and width of each background piece needed for the placemat. Remember to add ½" (1.3 cm) to both length and width for seam allowances. It's easiest to add extra and trim the section to size after assembly. When working with angled shapes, it's important to cut the background fabric even larger to accommodate the angle. Audition each piece before sewing to be sure it's large enough.

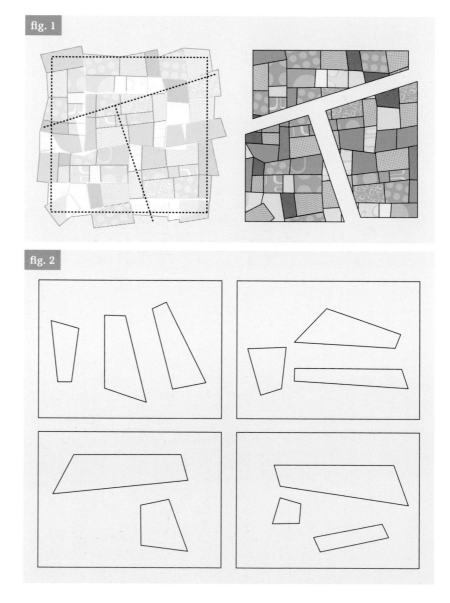

fig. 1

fig. 2

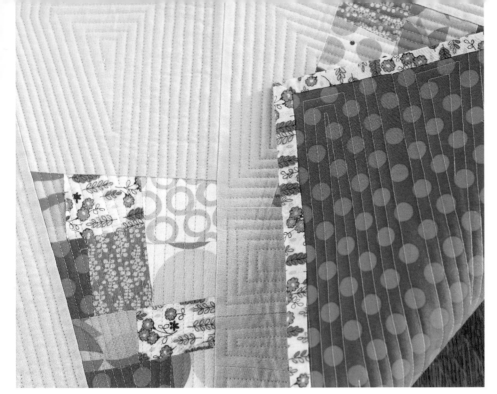

7   Cut and sew strips of background fabric to the top and bottom of the crazy-pieced shapes and press away from the crazy piecing. Trim the strips to align with the sides of the crazy-pieced shapes as shown in **fig. 3**.

8   Sew background strips to the sides of the crazy-pieced shapes. Work with the placemat as a whole; a single background strip can be sewn to the sides of two crazy-pieced sections, joining them together. Press seam allowances away from the crazy piecing. Trim the sewn unit to 14½" × 19½" (37 × 49.5 cm) **(fig. 4)**. Repeat Steps 4 through 7 to make three more placemat tops.

9   Cut four pieces of backing fabric and four pieces of batting, each 17" × 22" (43 × 56 cm). Make a quilt sandwich from one backing, one batting, and one placemat top. Repeat to make sandwiches for the other three placemats. Baste the layers together.

10 Quilt each placemat as desired. Trim the backing and batting even with the pieced top.

11 Join two binding strips to make the binding for each placemat. Bind the raw edges to finish the placemats. See chapter 4 (page 32) for further instructions on basting and binding.

On each placemat, dense straight-line quilting with lines ¼" (6 mm) apart echoes the crazy-pieced sections and the negative shapes that the background fabric forms. ✢

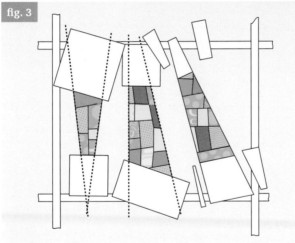

fig. 3

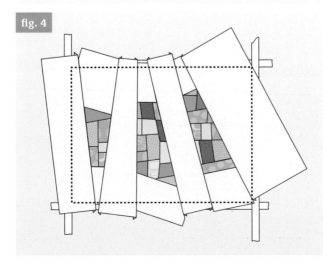

fig. 4

embrace your curves

IMPROVISATIONAL CURVES
TECHNIQUE AND PROJECTS

Curves are the proverbial thorn in the side of many quilters. Some of us hate to admit that we avoid curved piecing or that we view curves as finicky and difficult. With a little optimism and practice, curves, especially improvised curves, are manageable even for beginners. Free-pieced, free-cut curves require no templates, no pinning, and no stress. In our Improvisational Curve technique, curves are cut freehand with a rotary cutter and sewn without pinning, allowing you to create playful, modern quilts with curves.

◀ *Sardinia table runner, page 160*

improvisational curves technique

This technique allows you to sew what we call "gentle curves" with ease. To practice this technique, gather fabric scraps, a fabric marker, spray starch or Mary Ellen's Best Press spray-starch alternative, your rotary cutter, cutting mat, and acrylic quilter's rulers.

basic improvisational curves

1   Iron the fabric pieces with starch or Best Press to prepare fabric for cutting. Place a fresh sharp blade in your rotary cutter. Cut slowly and keep your other hand out of the way.

2   Cut two practice pieces: 5" × 10" (12.5 × 25.5 cm) piece A and 4" × 10" (10 × 25.5 cm) piece B.

3   Overlap A onto B with both fabrics right sides up, making the overlap wide enough to accommodate the desired curve. Cut your curve as shown in **fig. 1**. The gentler the curve, the easier it will be to sew. We cut without marking, but you can use a fabric marker to draw the curve first if you like.

4   You can also cut the gentle curves one fabric at a time. Cut the curve into A. Overlap A onto B to accommodate the curve; using the raw edge of A as a template, cut B along the curve. Discard the trimmings.

5   Mark fabric B where it meets the top right corner of A **(fig. 2)**. Flip A onto B so the right sides are together,

matching the top right corner of A with the mark on B. Pin at the mark to hold the fabrics together.

6   Turn the fabrics over and sew with B on top. Take the fabrics to the sewing machine, place under the presser foot, and lower the presser foot to hold the fabrics. Remove the pin.

7   Hold piece B with your left hand, lifting it up slightly. Guide piece A with your right hand. Your hands will be working independently.

8   Sew slowly, keeping the curved raw edges aligned under the presser foot. You'll have a natural tendency to force the two pieces to align

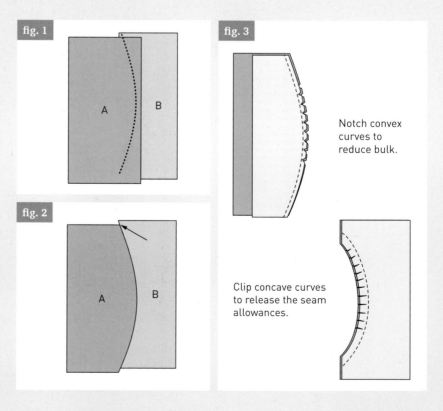

fig. 1

fig. 2

fig. 3

Notch convex curves to reduce bulk.

Clip concave curves to release the seam allowances.

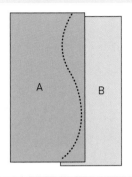

fig. 4

A   B

in front of the presser foot; resist that urge. Allow the pieces to ease into the presser foot and align as they move underneath.

9 Stop with the needle down and adjust your hand positions every few stitches. Remember to keep your left hand slightly elevated as you sew. Continue sewing the entire curve.

10 Press the seam to either side. For sharper curves you may need to clip the curve **(fig. 3)** to achieve a nice flat seam. Be sure not to clip into the stitches.

11 As you gain experience you'll be able to sew wavy curves like the one in **fig. 4**.

12 Practice sewing a few curves using this method before you start a project. You'll be sewing curves successfully in no time.

pods

1 Use the Improvisational Curve technique to piece the curved shapes we call pods. We've found the pod **(fig. 5)**, made with two improvised gentle curves that enclose a pod shape with background fabric, to be a versatile block to use in our projects.

2 To make a practice pod, cut a 2½" × 8" (6.5 × 20.5 cm) strip of fabric for the pod and two 3" × 11" (7.5 × 28 cm) strips of background fabric. Prepare the fabric for cutting by spraying with starch or Best Press and pressing. When making pods for your projects, be sure the background strip is at least 3" (7.5 cm) longer than the pod.

3 Cut a gentle curve through the pod fabric, beginning near the center of the bottom edge and ending at about the top center of the strip **(fig. 6)**. Curve close to the side edge for a wider finished pod.

4 Rotate the strip 180 degrees and cut the opposite side. Start the cut ¼" (6 mm) from the bottom left corner and end ¼" (6 mm) from the top left corner **(fig. 7)**.

5 Center the pod vertically on one background strip, with both fabrics right side up, as shown in **fig. 8**, with the background raw edge running through the center of the pod. Using the pod as a template, cut the same curve into the background fabric. Discard the small piece of background fabric underneath the pod.

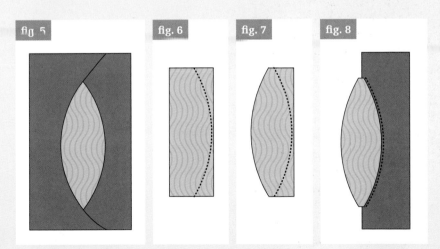

fig. 5   fig. 6   fig. 7   fig. 8

6   Lay the two pieces side by side and make a mark on the background fabric at the top right corner of the pod **(fig. 9)**.

7   Flip the pod right side down on the background fabric, matching its top right corner with the mark, and pin **(fig. 10)**.

8   Flip the pieces over and sew with background fabric on top. Put the needle down (into the fabric) and remove the pin before you sew. **Fig. 11** shows pod and background ready to sew.

9   Follow the instructions for sewing a gentle curve to sew the pod to the background. Press seam toward the pod.

10   Place the sewn piece on the second background strip as shown in **fig. 12**, with both pieces right side up. Make sure there is enough overlap to cover half the width of the pod. Cut the curve, following the edge of the pod. Start and end the cut on the background strips by extending the line of the curve as shown. Discard the excess fabric under the pod.

11   Repeat Steps 6 through 9 to sew on the second background strip. Press the seam away from the pod.

12   Trim the pod unit into a rectangle. Make the rectangle as wide and long as possible to allow flexibility when using the pod block in a project. You must have at least ¾" (2 cm) of background fabric on all sides of the pod.

fig. 9

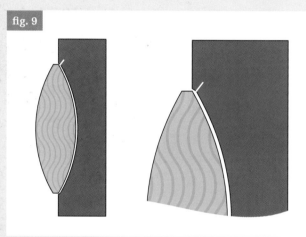

fig. 10

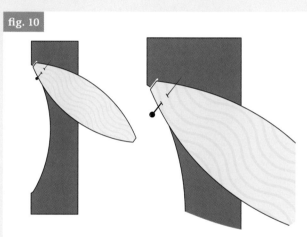

fig. 11

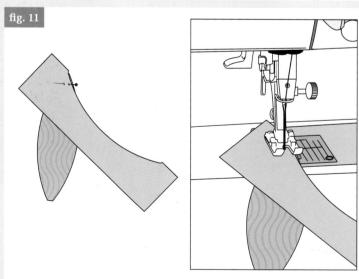

fig. 12

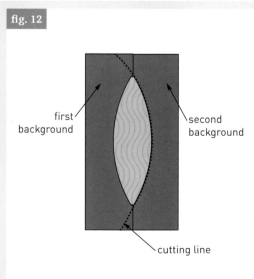

first background

second background

cutting line

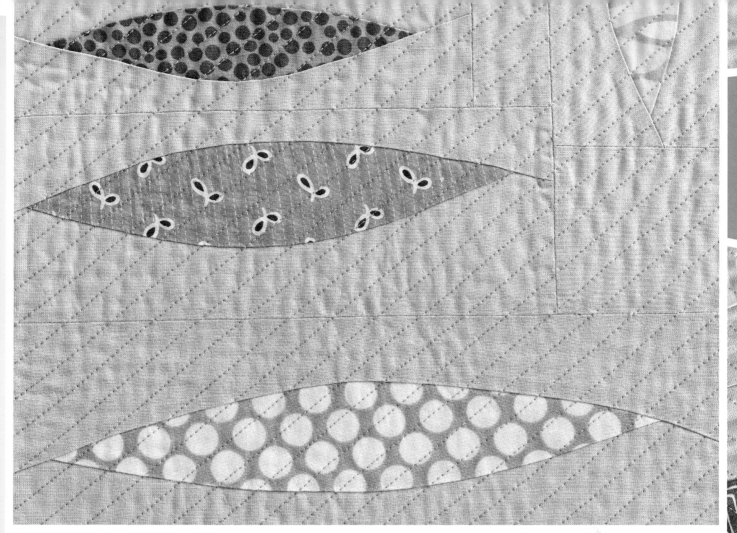

hints and tips

✛ Longer strips may be more challenging to cut. Take your time and cut slowly and carefully.

✛ Sewing curves freehand is counterintuitive since you'll naturally want to sew a straight line. Resist the urge to force the fabrics together.

✛ Keep the edge of the fabric aligned to the right of the needle and ¼" (6 mm) in front of the needle.

✛ Try not to watch the needle. Focus on the fabric edge about ¼" (6 mm) in front of the needle; in other words, where the needle will be falling next.

✛ Stop and adjust whenever you need to as you stitch a curve, even every two or three stitches. Leave the needle down, take a breath, and continue.

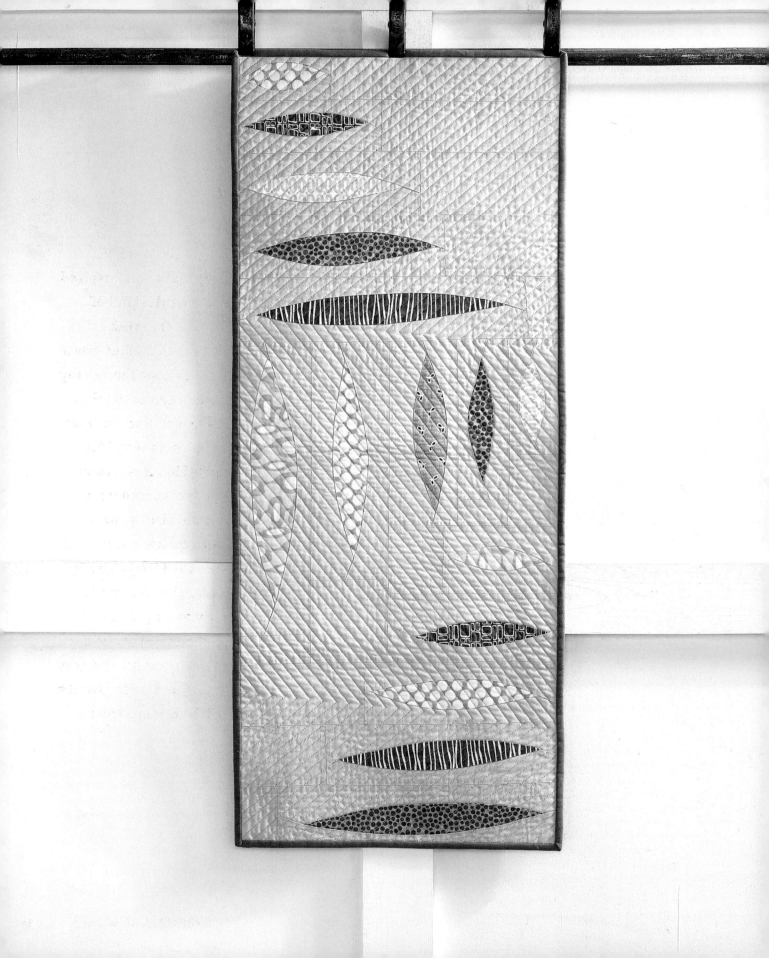

sardinia table runner

finished size: 16" × 39" (40.5 × 99 cm)

We wish we could tell you that this project was inspired by the beautiful island of Sardinia, but the truth is that Jacquie's husband saw a stack of pods near the sewing machine and remarked that the pods looked like sardines. We took it from there. The Sardinia table runner consists of fifteen free-pieced pods in graduated sizes placed vertically and horizontally in the piece. The free-cut pods create a fanciful feeling in an orderly arrangement. The touch of yellow provides a splash of color, while the gray background and pods give the piece a subtle, muted feel.

materials
All fabric amounts are for 45" (114.5 cm) wide fabric.

- 1 fat eighth each of 5 different yellow and gray prints (If fat eighths aren't available, substitute ⅛ yd [11.4 cm] full-width cuts.)
- 1¼ yd (114.5 cm) gray fabric for background
- ⅝ yd (57 cm) fabric for backing
- ¼ yd (23 cm) fabric for binding
- 20" × 42" (51 × 106.5 cm) low-loft cotton batting

tools
- Modern quilter's toolbox (page 10)
- New rotary cutter blade
- Spray starch or Mary Ellen's Best Press spray-starch alternative

cut the fabric

* From background fabric, cut 9 strips 3" (7.5 cm) × width of fabric.

* From gray and yellow print fabrics, cut the following for the pods, using 3 different prints for each set of same-sized strips:

  › 3 strips 12" × 2½" (30.5 × 6.5 cm)

  › 3 strips 10" × 2½" (25.5 × 6.5 cm)

  › 3 strips 8" × 2½" (20.5 × 6.5 cm)

  › 3 strips 6" × 2½" (15 × 6.5 cm)

  › 3 strips 4" × 2½" (10 × 6.5 cm).

* From binding fabric, cut 3 strips 2¼" (5.5 cm) × width of fabric.

construct the quilt

Note: Unless otherwise indicated, all seam allowances are ¼" (6 mm) and are pressed open.

1 See page 157 for detailed instructions for cutting pods and making pod blocks.

2 Press and starch the strips for the pods and the background rectangles. Place a fresh blade in your rotary cutter and remember to cut slowly and carefully as you cut freehand.

3 Cut fifteen pods from the print fabric strips. Make some pods skinny, some fat, and some in between, but all should be at least 1½" (3.8 cm) wide at the widest point. Arrange the pods in stacks by size **(fig. 1)**.

4 For each pod, cut two rectangles from the 3" (7.5 cm) background strips, each at least 3" (7.5 cm) longer than the pod. Surround each pod

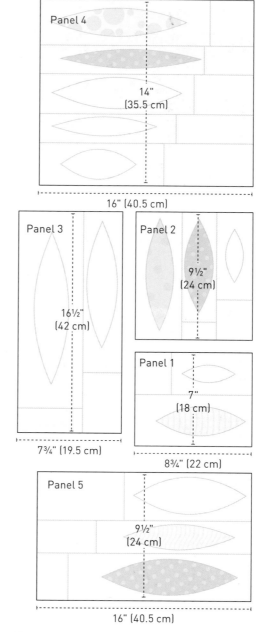

Panel measurements are prior to joining the panels.
Your measurements may differ depending on the size of your pods.

Sardinia Runner construction diagram

with background fabric to make fifteen pod blocks.

5 Trim the pod blocks into rectangles **(fig. 2)**. Make the rectangles as wide and long as possible to allow flexibility while assembling the table runner. Be sure to leave at

least ¾" (2 cm) of background fabric on all sides of the pod.

6 Place the pod blocks on the design wall according to the construction diagram above.

7 The table runner is constructed from five panels.

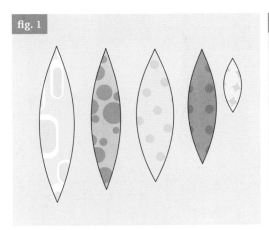

fig. 1

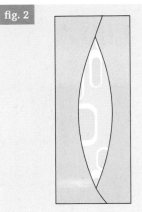

fig. 2

Begin by adding background-fabric extensions to pod blocks, then join those units together to form the panels. Remember to take seam allowances into account when cutting extensions for the pod blocks.

8 To create panel 1, add background fabric to the left side of the top pod in the panel, extending the pod to equal the measurement of the pod below. Sew the two pods together.

9 Measure the longest pod of panel 2. Extend the two smaller pods in panel 2 so they both measure the same length as the longest pod. Don't sew these pod blocks together yet.

10 Measure the widths of the three pod blocks in panel 2 without seam allowances. Extend or trim the three panels so that, when sewn together, they will equal the width of panel 1.

11 Sew the three panel 2 pod blocks together.

12 Sew panels 1 and 2 together. Measure the length of this new section. Extend the two pod

blocks in panel 3 to equal this measurement.

13 Sew panel 3 to the panel 1+2 unit. Measure the width of this new section to determine the final width of the table runner.

14 Using background fabric, extend all the pod blocks in panels 4 and 5 to the width of the table runner. Sew the pod blocks together to create panels 4 and 5.

15 Sew panel 4 to the top of the center section and sew panel 5 to the bottom of the center section.

16 Make a quilt sandwich from the backing, batting, and runner top. Baste the layers together.

17 Quilt as desired. Trim the backing and batting to match the pieced runner top.

18 Join the binding strips to make a continuous length. Bind the raw edges to finish the runner. See chapter 4 (page 32) for further instructions on basting and binding.

Simple straight-line quilting adds texture and movement to the runner. We established a diagonal through the center pod group and two diagonals at right angles in opposite directions, then quilted straight lines echoing the angles at ½" (1.3 cm) intervals, filling the entire runner. ✦

calculate extension lengths

To calculate extension lengths, use this formula:

- Final length required minus length of pod block (without seam allowances) = X
- X + ½" (1.3 cm) seam allowance = minimum length of strip to cut

For a 12" (30.5 cm) pod block that needs to be extended to 16" (40.5 cm) long, the formula works like this:

- 16" − 12" = 4" (40.5 − 30.5 = 10 cm), and
- 4" + ½" = 4½" (10 + 1.5 = 11.5 cm)
- Add a 4½" (11.5 cm) extension to get the required length.

We like to add a bit extra to our extensions and then trim back, so the extension could be cut 5" to 6" (12.5 to 15 cm) long.

tipsy city quilt

finished size: 31" × 35" (79 cm × 89 cm)

We are both city girls. We thrive on the energy and activity of a bustling city. In the Tipsy City quilt we attempted to capture that energetic feeling with vibrant, saturated colors and the dynamic movement of curves. Simple improvised blocks combine to create towers, and gentle curves create a whimsical, tilted cityscape. The result is an exceptionally bright and dramatic quilt in a size that's ideal for wall or baby.

materials

All fabric amounts are for 45" (114.5 cm) wide fabric unless otherwise listed.

- 1 yd (91.5 cm) cerise (reddish-purple) fabric for background
- ¼ yd (23 cm) light blue fabric
- 1 fat quarter (18" × 22" [45.5 × 56 cm]) or ¼ yd (23 cm) cut of each:

  - Aqua
  - Orange
  - Violet
  - Gold
  - Light orange
  - Gray
  - Turquoise
  - Burnt orange
  - Lime green

- 1⅛ yd (103 cm) fabric for backing
- ⅓ yd (30.5 cm) fabric for binding
- 39" × 43" (99 × 109 cm) low-loft cotton batting

tools

- Modern quilter's toolbox (page 10)

cut the fabric

✳ From cerise background fabric, cut:

  → 1 strip 12" (30.5 cm) × width of fabric

  → 2 strips 6" × 28" (15 × 71 cm).

✳ From binding fabric, cut 4 strips 2¼" (5.5 cm) × width of fabric.

construct the quilt

Note: Unless otherwise indicated, all seam allowances are ¼" (6 mm) and are pressed open.

1 Tipsy City consists of four "towers" of improvised blocks **(fig. 1)** based on the Courthouse Steps Log Cabin variation. Each tower is about 24" (61 cm) tall and 5½" (14 cm) wide. Build your towers one block at a time. To begin, gather the nine solid-color fabrics near the cutting mat. Cut strips from these fabrics as needed to make the tower blocks. The width of the strips will depend on the size of each block's center; each block must be at least 5½" (14 cm) wide when finished. Remember the loss from seam allowances when calculating the strip widths.

2 Make three tower blocks and sew them together along their 5½" (14 cm) sides to make a tower. Measure the height of the three-block tower **(fig. 2)**. Subtract that height from 25" (63.5 cm); the result is the necessary height for the final block in the tower. Make the last block, cutting the first two contrasting-fabric strips to yield the necessary height, and sew it to the bottom of the tower.

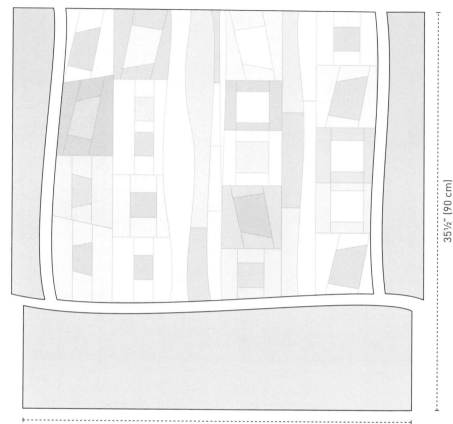

Tipsy City construction diagram

31" (79 cm)

35½" (90 cm)

3 Towers may have as many tower and/or double blocks (see page 169) as desired, as long as the tower is about 25" (63.5 cm) high. Our blocks range from 5½" × 5½" (14 × 14 cm) to 5½" × 8½" (14 × 21.5 cm). Blocks can be sewn together traditionally or angle pieced with the method described on page 50. With this angle-piecing method, the blocks will maintain straight sides so you can add additional blocks without trimming **(fig. 3)**. Make four towers, each 25" (63.5 cm) high.

4 Make at least five strips, each 4½" (11.5 cm) to 6" (15 cm)

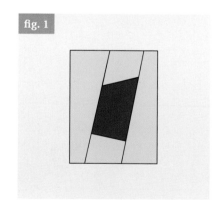

fig. 1

wide and 28" (71 cm) long, to use as columns between the towers. These strips can be a single color or pieced. Follow our color placement or create your own.

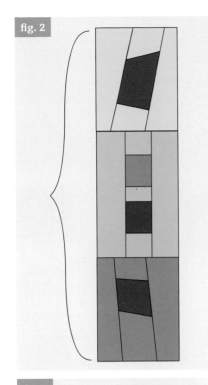

fig. 2

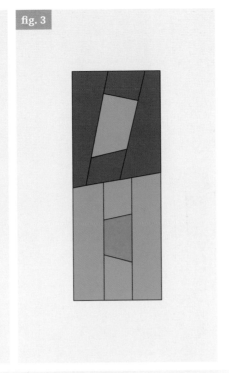

fig. 3

5   Arrange the towers and column strips on the design wall in order **(fig. 4)**. Decide where you want straight seams and where you'd like to join pieces with gentle curves. We used both.

6   Because these columns are tall, the freehand curves joining them will be very long. Consider drawing the curve with a fabric marker before cutting. Overlap two pieces to be joined, being sure that both pieces are right side up, cut the curve, and sew. Press the curved seams to one side.

fig. 4

7 Where the curves make a large lateral shift, add partial strips in the same way to fill any gaps. Overlap the two strips, right sides up, to accommodate the curve **(fig. 5)**, cut the curve, and sew. Treat this strip pair as a single column.

8 Repeat Steps 6 and 7 to join all the columns and towers. Add a 6" (15 cm) cerise strip to each side of the assembled unit with gently curved seams. Square and trim the piece so all the outer corners are right angles.

9 Sew the 12" (30.5 cm) cerise strip to the bottom of the pieced unit with a gently curved seam, centering the tower unit from side to side. Trim the sides of the cerise strip to square and straighten the quilt top.

10 Measure the quilt top. Cut the backing fabric and batting 8" (20.5 cm) longer and wider than the top.

11 Make a quilt sandwich from the backing, batting, and quilt top. Baste the layers together.

12 Quilt as desired. Trim the backing and batting to match the quilt top.

13 Join the binding strips to make a continuous length. Bind the raw edges to finish the quilt. See chapter 4 (page 32) for further instructions on basting and binding.

Note: Our binding is broken by a strip of improvisational piecing along one side of the quilt. To achieve this effect, piece fabric scraps from the quilt top together and trim them to make a 2¼" (5.5 cm) wide strip. Place the pieced strip between two of the solid binding strips when joining them end to end, then attach the binding as usual.

We quilted the Tipsy City quilt's curvy lines using a sewing machine with a walking foot attachment. Some of the lines echo the edges of the gentle curves in the piecing and others curve randomly in the towers and the columns. ✛

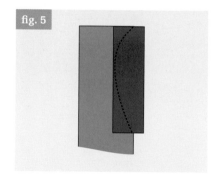

fig. 5

tower block construction

1 | Cut a four-sided shape for the center about 2" (5 cm) wide and up to 4" (10 cm) tall.

2 | Add strips of a contrasting color above and below the center. Trim the strips along the center's sides **(fig. 6)**.

3 | Sew strips of the same contrasting color to the sides of the unit. Square and trim the block to 5½" (14 cm) wide and between 5½" (14 cm) and 8½" (21.5 cm) tall **(fig. 7)**.

4 | For variety, make one or more double blocks by using two centers and sewing a strip between them **(fig. 8)**. Finish the block as directed above.

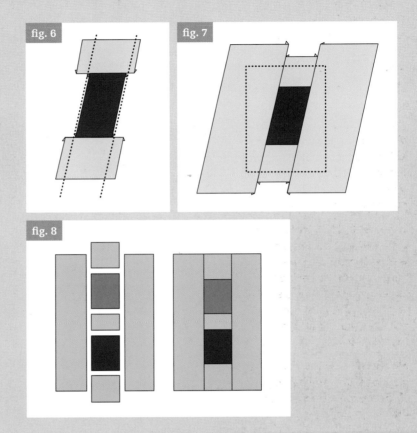

fig. 6

fig. 7

fig. 8

iLLusions QuiLt

finished size: 48½" × 56½" (122 × 142 cm)

Serendipity sometimes plays a role in improvisational quilting. The Illusions quilt is an example of one of those happy accidents that occur in the studio. The design emerged as we experimented with improvised pod blocks. The fabrics and the positions of the blocks create multiple designs, including the propellers, a skewed diamond where the four triangles come together, and the illusion of circles formed by the yellow background fabric.

materials

All fabric amounts are for 45" (114.5 cm) wide fabric.

- 2⅞ yd (2.6 m) light yellow fabric for background
- 1 fat quarter (18" × 22" [45.5 × 56 cm]) or ⅜ yd (34.3 cm) each of 14 different black-and-white prints, half light values and half dark
- 3⅛ yd (2.9 m) fabric for backing
- ½ yd (45.5 cm) fabric for binding
- 56½" × 64½" (143.5 × 164 cm) low-loft cotton batting

tools

- Modern quilter's toolbox (page 10)
- 8½" (21.5 cm) squaring ruler
- New rotary cutter blade
- Spray starch or Mary Ellen's Best Press spray-starch alternative

cut the fabric

✳ From light yellow fabric, cut 7 strips 14" (35.5 cm) × width of fabric, then cross-cut these strips into 84 rectangles, each 3" × 14" (7.5 × 35.5 cm).

✳ From each of the black-and-white print fabrics, cut:

  ▸ 3 squares 7½" × 7½" (19 × 19 cm) (42 total)

  ▸ 3 rectangles 4" × 9" (10 × 23 cm) rectangles (42 total).

✳ From binding fabric, cut 6 strips 2¼" (5.5 cm) × width of fabric.

✳ From backing fabric, cut 2 lengths, each 56" (142 cm).

construct the quilt

Note: Unless otherwise indicated, all seam allowances are ¼" (6 mm) and are pressed open.

1 See page 157 for instructions for cutting pods and making pod blocks.

2 Press and starch the black-and-white rectangles for the pods and the yellow background rectangles. Place a fresh blade in your rotary cutter and remember to work slowly and carefully as you cut freehand.

3 Cut forty-two pods from the 4" × 9" (10 × 23 cm) black-and-white rectangles. The pods should be at least 2½" (6.5 cm) wide at their widest point.

4 Surround each black-and-white pod with yellow background fabric to make forty-two pod blocks **(fig. 1)**. Trim to the largest rectangle possible, at least 12½" (31.5 cm) long.

Each block measures 8½" (21.5 cm) square before blocks are joined.

Illusions construction diagram

5 Cut the forty-two black-and-white 7½" (19 cm) squares in half on the diagonal to make eighty-four triangles. Sort the triangles by value in two stacks, one light and one dark.

6 Sew a light-value triangle to one side of a pod block, aligning their centers **(fig. 2)**. Press the seam open. Repeat for all forty-two of the pod blocks. Chain piece if desired.

7 Repeat Step 6 to sew a dark-value triangle to the opposite side of all forty-two pod blocks.

8 Trim all the blocks to 8½" (21.5 cm) square **(fig. 3)**.

9 Arrange the forty-two blocks on the design wall according to the construction diagram above, alternating light- and dark-value triangles to form the diamonds.

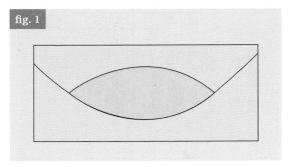

fig. 1

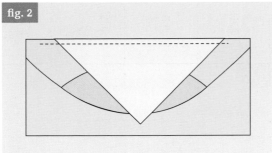

fig. 2

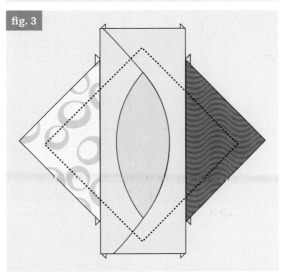

fig. 3

10 Sew the blocks together in order from left to right to form rows. Place each completed row back on the design wall in the correct position.

11 Sew rows in order from top to bottom, matching seams and aligning raw edges, to complete the quilt top.

12 Trim the selvedges from the backing fabric. Sew the pieces together along one long edge and trim to 56" × 64" (142 × 162.5 cm).

13 Make a quilt sandwich from the backing, batting, and quilt top. Baste the layers together.

14 Quilt as desired. Trim the backing and batting to match the quilt top.

15 Join the binding strips to make a continuous length. Bind the raw edges to finish the quilt. See chapter 4 (page 32) for further instructions on basting and binding.

We quilted the Illusions quilt to emphasize the curves that occur in the quilt. Quilting echoes the curved pods, and each pod is quilted with repeating arcs. A curvy floral motif fills the skewed diamonds. ✛

resources

The materials and tools used to make the projects in this book are readily available from local quilt shops, large sewing retailers, and online retailers. Here are a few of our favorite sources.

fabric and quilting supplies

Cia's Palette
ciaspalette.com
Fabric essentials for quilters.

The Colorwheel Company
colorwheelco.com
Pocket colorwheel.

Jo-Ann Fabrics and Crafts
joann.com
Osnaburg, fabrics, batting, and a full range of quilting supplies.

Marmalade Fabrics
marmaladefabrics.com
Quilting fabrics and supplies.

Pink Chalk Fabrics
pinkchalkfabrics.com
Quilting fabrics and supplies.

Robert Kaufman Fabrics
robertkaufman.com
Makers of Carolina chambray solid, Kona cotton solids, cotton broadcloth, Essex linen and cotton blend, Aiden linen, and Waterford linen.

The Warm Company
warmcompany.com
Makers of quilt batting, including Warm and Natural, Warm and White, and Insulbrite.

Westminster Fabrics
westminsterfabrics.com
Solid fabrics, woven fabrics, and shot cottons.

additional quilting resources

Angela Walters
quiltingismytherapy.com
ange_walters1@yahoo.com
Custom long-arm quilting.

Mary Ellen Products
maryellenproducts.com
Best Press clear spray-starch alternative and other products.

Quilter's Touch
quilterstouch.com
Machingers Quilting Gloves and other products.

Day Style Designs
daystyledesigns.com
Free Motion Quilting Basics for Beginners DVD and other supplies.

author blogs

Tallgrass Prairie Studio
tallgrassprairiestudio.blogspot.com
Jacquie Gering

Sew Katie Did
sewkatiedid.wordpress.com
Katie Pedersen

inspirational modern quilting blogs

Bumble Beans
bumblebeansinc.blogspot.com
Victoria Findlay Wolfe

Film in the Fridge
filminthefridge.com
Ashley Williamson

Handmade by Alissa
handmadebyalissa.com
Alissa Haight-Carlton

Naptime Quilter
naptimequilter.blogspot.com
Cheryl Arkison

Oh Fransson
ohfransson.com
Elizabeth Hartman

One Shabby Chick
oneshabbychick.typepad.com
Amber Carillio

The Silly Boo Dilly
thesillyboodilly.blogspot.com
Victoria Gertenbach

Syko
syko.typepad.com
Kajsa Wikman

True Up
trueup.net
Kim Knight

recommended reading

Fahl, Ann. *Dancing with Thread: Your Guide to Free-Motion Quilting.* Lafayette, California: C&T Publishing, 2010.

Noble, Maurine. *Machine Quilting Made Easy.* Bothell, Washington: Martingale & Co., 1994.

index

Looking for more books on modern quilting?
Check out these inspiring resources from Interweave

Fresh Quilting
Fearless Color, Design, and Inspiration

Malka Dubrawsky

ISBN 978-1-59668-235-1
$26.95

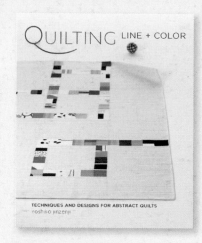

Quilting Line + Color
Techniques and Designs for Abstract Quilts

Yoshiko Jinzenji

ISBN 978-1-59668-333-4
$28.95

I Love Patchwork!
21 Irresistible Zakka Projects to Sew

Rashida Coleman Hale

ISBN 978-1-59668-142-2
$24.95

Quilting Arts
MAGAZINE®

Whether you consider yourself a contemporary quilter, fiber artist, art quilter, embellished quilter, or wearable art artist, *Quilting Arts Magazine* strives to meet your creative needs. **Quiltingdaily.com**

Quilting Daily

Quiltingdaily.com, the online contemporary quilting community, offers free patterns, expert tips and techniques, e-newsletters, blogs, forums, videos, special offers, and more! **Quiltingdaily.com**

Quilting Daily shop
shop.quiltingdaily.com